THE NATIONAL ASSOCIATION REALTORS

GUIDE TO

Home Selling

THE NATIONAL ASSOCIATION OF REALTORS®

GUIDE TO

Home Selling

NATIONAL ASSOCIATION OF REALTORS®

The Voice for Real Estate®

with **Blanche Evans**

BICENTENNIAL
1807
WILEY
2007
BICENTENNIAL

John Wiley & Sons, Inc.

For general information on our other products and services or for technical support, please contact our Customer Care Department within the United States at (800) 762-2974, outside the United States at (317) 572-3993 or fax (317) 572-4002.

Wiley also publishes its books in a variety of electronic formats. Some content that appears in print may not be available in electronic books. For more information about Wiley products, visit our web site at www.wiley.com.

Library of Congress Cataloging-in-Publication Data:

The National Association of Realtors® guide to home selling / The National
Association of Realtors® with Blanche Evans.
    p. cm.
  ISBN-13: 978-0-470-03790-4 (pbk.)
  ISBN-10: 0-470-03790-3 (pbk.)
    1. House selling—United States. I. Evans, Blanche. II. National Association
of Realtors.
HD259.N362 2007
643'.120973—dc22

                    2006015379

Printed in the United States of America.

10 9 8 7 6 5 4 3 2 1

Contents

Acknowledgments

The NATIONAL ASSOCIATION OF REALTORS® thanks Blanche Evans for her time, expertise, and dedication to this project.

NAR would like to thank the following people for their valuable contributions in the creation of this publication: Bob Goldberg, Laurie Janik, David Lereah, Frank Sibley, Pat Kaplan, Pamela Williams, Matt Lombardi, Ken Burlington, Mary Martinez, Thomas Doyle, Dan Schmitz, Peggy Selinger-Eaton, David Knox, and Larry Jellen. NAR also thanks the following groups for their support: the Real Estate Buyer's Agent Council (REBAC); the staff at REALTOR® Magazine Online; and Jody Lane and the staff at *Realty Times*.

In addition, special thanks go to our editor, Laurie Harting, and the team at John Wiley & Sons for all of their support for this project.

Blanche Evans would like to thank the wonderful staff at the NATIONAL ASSOCIATION OF REALTORS®, specifically Ken Burlington, Pamela Williams, Bob Goldberg, Frank Sibley, Stacey Moncrieff, and Steve Cook, with special kudos to Chief Economist David Lereah and his fine research staff.

Special thanks also goes to Jody Lane, founder of *Realty Times*, *Realty Times TV*, and RealtyTimes.com. Without his support and encouragement, and occasional borrowing of the services of our terrific copy editor, Carla Davis, this project would not have been possible.

Laurie Harting of John Wiley & Sons has been a delight, and her guidance and ability to keep everyone on schedule and on track are appreciated.

It is an honor beyond imagining to be able to provide the voice for "The Voice for Real Estate®"—The NATIONAL ASSOCIATION OF REALTORS®.

Introduction

Whether this is the first time—or the fifth—that you are selling a home, there's information you need to know and there are steps you need to take to ensure you receive the best possible offer.

The NATIONAL ASSOCIATION OF REALTORS® Guide to Home Selling is a user-friendly, informative, and concise book designed to guide you through the process of selling your home using the professional knowledge and experience of the largest home-owner lobbying group and trade organization in the world—the NATIONAL ASSOCIATION OF REALTORS® (NAR).

NAR has partnered with respected real estate journalist Blanche Evans, editor of *Realty Times* (www.realtytimes.com), the Internet's largest real estate news and advice source, to bring you the most objective and resourceful guide to home selling possible.

This comprehensive guide provides you with important questions you need to ask yourself and options you need to consider as you go through the home selling process, including:

- Deciding when it's right to sell your home.
- Hiring the right listing agent.
- Preparing your home for showings and open houses.
- Staging your home for maximum impact.
- Understanding how real estate markets work.
- Setting the right price for your home.
- Working with offers.
- Finalizing a deal.
- Closing on the sale of your home.
- Moving day tips.

Use the tips and tricks in this book to help you understand the entire process to get the best offer when you sell your home.

What You Will Learn from This Book

You'll examine the reasons you've decided to sell your home and determine the financial impact of your decision.

You'll learn how to choose the right real estate listing agent and what to look for in a marketing plan for selling your home.

You'll learn the importance of preparing your home to put it on the market and the importance of curb appeal. You'll learn about the benefits of staging your home to appeal to buyers' imaginations and whether extensive remodeling jobs will actually increase the value of your home.

You'll learn about housing markets and some of the motivations of buyers in the purchasing process. You'll learn realistic strategies for setting the price to get the most money possible for your home.

You'll learn about the methods buyers use to find properties, and how you and your agent should apply them to your marketing plan to get the best exposure of your home to buyers on the market.

You'll learn about the offer process and what to expect from buyers as they make offers on your home.

You'll review the steps of the closing process and understand where problems and delays can arise if you aren't prepared.

Finally, moving day will come. You'll finish with easy tips for moving into your new home.

So sit back, get out your highlighter, and let the real estate experts help you get started using the latest and most effective home selling techniques!

About the NATIONAL ASSOCIATION OF REALTORS®

The NATIONAL ASSOCIATION OF REALTORS®, "The Voice for Real Estate®," is the largest trade organization in the United States, with more than 1.2 million members. Membership is composed of residential and commercial members who are brokers, salespeople, property managers, appraisers, counselors, and other related professionals.

The term REALTOR® is a registered membership mark. Only NAR members are allowed to call themselves REALTORS®, and to wear and display the easily recognizable blue REALTOR® R. As members, they've committed to abide by NAR's strict Code of Ethics and Standards of Practice.

What does that mean to you? While its mission is to help its members become more profitable and successful, NAR is also intent on raising the standard of professional practice, ethics, and behavior for its members to follow. Consumers should know the difference and ask their agents if they are "REALTORS®."

Since 1908, NAR has influenced the buying and selling of real estate in profound ways by providing facilities for professional development, research, and communication between the industry and the public and government. Without NAR, the free enterprise system with regard to the right to own, use, and transfer real property might be more expensive and offer far fewer benefits to owners than it does now.

Composed primarily of state-licensed real estate agents and brokers, NAR has three organizational levels—local, state, and national. Members belong to more than 1,400 local associations/boards in 54 states and territories.

REALTORS® use their membership clout to lobby for homeowner and industry issues at all levels. Many of the homeowner benefits today are a direct result of lobbying efforts by NAR, including:

- Federal tax relief and homeowner incentives (Tax Relief Act of 1997).
- Mortgage interest rate deductions.
- Lower real estate taxes.
- Local tax benefits.
- Low-income assistance programs.
- Higher ceilings on federally insured loans for expensive markets.
- Tax-free gains on primary residences, owner-occupied two out of five years—$500,000 for married couples, $250,000 for singles.
- Protections from mortgage fraud and predatory lending.
- Freedom of choice in real estate agent selection and type of representation.

The list goes on and on. So remember, when you hire a REALTOR®, you're really putting the strength of more than 1.2 million members in your corner.

Why Use a REALTOR®?

Over 85 percent of consumers use a real estate agent to buy or sell their homes. That's because buying or selling a home is one of the biggest financial challenges any consumer is likely to ever make. While the rewards are great, there are a number of financial and legal risks attached to owning and selling property. A REALTOR® can help you avoid pitfalls that could otherwise unravel a deal to sell your home.

Your agent is equipped to help you list and market your home to attract the largest number of potential buyers. Your agent should use a wide variety of tools, from his/her association membership and access to the local multiple listing service (MLS), to Internet and direct mail marketing and advertising, to networking with fellow agents, clients, and contacts to advertise your home to the largest audience possible. She or he will help you negotiate terms that are favorable for your finances, your moving date, and your goals.

Depending on the relationship you develop with your agent, you might find that some go much further, including helping you to find the next home you want to live in, finding you service technicians, and much more that isn't part of an agent's usual services.

In choosing a REALTOR®, you will have an agent who is committed to NAR's strict Code of Ethics, which is based on professionalism and protection of the public. That's why all real estate licensees are not the same. Ongoing ethics training is a mandatory requirement of NAR and a good way for you to know that your agent is accountable for his or her actions through disciplinary sanctions beyond those provided at the state and/or local level.

NAR members are required to be honest and ethical to all parties involved in the transaction whether it is the seller, buyer, or cooperating agent. REALTORS® build their business on their reputations. The greatest honor you can do for your REALTOR® is to recommend him or her to your friends and family.

About Blanche Evans and *Realty Times*

Since 1997, Blanche Evans and *Realty Times* (www.realtytimes.com) have been the Internet source for consumer and industry real estate news and advice. Independently owned and operated, *Realty Times* is not only a leading content provider, it is also the sponsor of *Realty Times TV*, which provides home buying and selling news and advice to consumers while showcasing REALTOR® listings from around the country.

Blanche Evans is the editor of *Realty Times* and a contributor to *Realty Times TV*. She has been recognized by the editors of *REALTOR® Magazine* as one of the 25 Most Influential People in Real Estate, and one of the few women recognized at the Notable level or above more than once. She is the author of numerous books, magazine articles, and white papers about the real estate industry, and is a well-received speaker at industry events. She is frequently interviewed by the media about consumer real estate issues and is widely regarded as one of the most knowledgeable people in the industry.

Realty Times is not associated with NAR, but over the years, the two organizations have found they have objectives in common—the desire to serve consumers while promoting higher industry standards.

THE NATIONAL
ASSOCIATION OF
REALTORS®

GUIDE TO
Home Selling

CHAPTER 1

It's Time to Sell

Making the decision to move can take you through a gauntlet of emotions—joy, fear, excitement, and anticipation. Naturally, you want to have the most positive experience possible in selling your home. A lot depends on why you're moving and how to optimize the sale.

Perhaps you're getting married, and you want to trade in your small condo for a house with a yard and a bath and closet built for two. Or, now that you've had kids, you find yourself in a home that is no longer a good fit. You want or need more space. Or it's time to downsize now that your children have emptied the nest.

You want to travel and go out to plays, clubs, and galleries, instead of staying home caring for a big yard.

These are fun reasons to move because you get the opportunity to choose a new home to suit the needs of your family and your pocketbook.

Some moves aren't so happy, however. You may be forced to sell because your company is transferring you or you've lost your job. Perhaps you're going through a divorce or the death of a spouse.

Whatever your reason, there's a proven strategy for success that can ease your burdens throughout the process and help you negotiate the best terms and price for your home.

Why Do Buyers Buy?

The first thing to do is recognize the three biggest reasons buyers purchase homes:

1. Location.
2. Condition.
3. Price.

Location

Location is another way of looking at vantage points. Most buyers want to be near work, schools, relatives and friends, or neighborhood amenities, but most important, they want to be in a quality neighborhood.

According to NAR's research, two-thirds of surveyed home buyers said that the quality of the neighborhood was the most important factor in choosing a home, followed by proximity to job or school (43 percent) and proximity to friends or family (36 percent).

Thirty-five percent of buyers reported that they did not make any compromises in general on factors such as neighborhood quality or the size of their home when making their purchase. When they did compromise, it was over the size of the home and price.

Condition

The condition of the home reflects the care that the homeowner has given the property. If a home is in prime condition—with no visible repairs needed, fresh paint, updated appliances, and air-conditioning systems—there is little reason for the buyer to complain about condition.

Size is important to home buyers, and many consider size to be closely related to condition. If a home is too small for a modern family's needs, it can be awkward to live in as well as difficult to decorate. Even though family sizes are smaller, home sizes have doubled since 1950, largely due to changes in society from working mothers to mass consumerism. Both parents work, often at opposite ends of town, so both need cars to park in two- or three-car garages. We own more personal belongings so we need bigger closets and more storage space. We engage in more activities than families of decades ago so we have more need for personal space. Societal changes are effectively making small homes functionally obsolete. As proof, 60 percent of home buyers bought homes that were 10 years old or less in 2005. The most typical home purchased in 2005 was more than 1,800 square feet.

Price

Home buyers want the most square footage and amenities that they can possibly get for the price. They tend to view properties as either wholesale or retail priced. A home that is in need of updates and maintenance will likely sell at "wholesale," because the buyer knows that in order to bring the house to modern standards, they will have to shoulder the cost that the seller deferred. If the home is in top condition, the buyer is likely to pay "retail," or top dollar for the neighborhood and homes.

Most buyers pay close to the original asking price, as price is a reflection of location and condition. In fact, NAR research shows that the median sales price was 99 percent of the original listing price.

Conversely, there is no statistical survey that outlines why homes don't sell, but almost any agent will tell you the number one reason homes don't sell is price. Price is related to a number of factors, and anything that turns off the buyer is going to impact price. Among these reasons are:

- Competition from newer, better homes or neighborhoods.
- Functional obsolescence.
- Stains, smells, and breakage.

Competition from Newer Homes and Neighborhoods. Buyers like to be on the cutting edge and are attracted to newly constructed homes in the same way that car buyers like that new car smell. Newer homes can offer design and neighborhood features that accommodate modern preferences, such as the use of home technologies or community recreational facilities for residents' use only.

Existing homes can still compete very well, because they may be closer to central business districts or offer unique architecture and charm such as Tudor and Cape Cod cottages or Colonial or Victorian mansions.

Human beings are migratory by nature and are always on the lookout for greener pastures, so they create desirability in neighborhoods and in certain types of homes. That can make one neighborhood soar in value while another nearby neighborhood appears to stagnate despite nearly identical advantages. You may also see some types of housing come back into vogue. Witness the phenomenal success of warehouse lofts and townhomes as home buyers return to inner cities.

Functional Obsolescence. Neighborhoods and houses are some-what like the rings of a tree that show their age. Existing homes reflect the home buyer preferences and living customs of their day.

As mentioned earlier, functional obsolescence can occur in home sizes, and it can also occur in floor plans. In the 1950s, the kitchen was the mom's retreat; today it's the gathering place for the family, so kitchens have enlarged. Master bedrooms have been separated from children's and guest suites. Today, many families need home offices more than they need formal living rooms. Some buyers may consider homes to be outdated if they are too small, awk-ward, or have the wrong rooms or other features that no longer apply to modern life.

Stains, Smells, and Breakage. Buyers don't like to be reminded that a home has been roughly used. The origin of grime is some-times not obvious, but pet stains and food stains on rugs are among the most unappealing to buyers. Water marks on walls and ceilings suggest that systems are failing and might be very expen-sive to fix, as well as indicating that there may be a mold problem.

The simple truth is that homes, like anything else that is regularly used, show signs of wear and tear. Buyers like those signs re-moved, or they will try to discount the home beyond the cost of the repair to pay for their trouble and any other unforeseen expenses.

It always pays to put your home in as near-perfect condition as you can so you can capture the highest price possible. A favorite saying of real estate agents is "You can't live in a home the way you sell a home." In other words, buyers need to see your home in beautiful form, free of clutter and life's inconveniences so they can envision themselves and their lifestyle in the home.

Upsizing, Downsizing, or Changing Your Lifestyle

When home sellers repurchase, they may buy a larger or a smaller home. This decision is most often based on whether there are school-age children living at home, whether there is extended family present such as aging parents to care for, and whether more or less space (and maintenance) is required for future lifestyle choices.

Before you decide to put your home on the market, be clear about what you want to accomplish, so you can budget accordingly.

If you are like half of all other sellers, you're moving up to a larger home. The choice of whether to move up or downsize is closely related to your age. If you're under 54, you're more likely to trade up. If you are older, you're more likely to downsize. A majority of home seller households (59 percent, according to NAR) have no children under the age of 18 living at home, but keep in mind that downsizing doesn't necessarily mean moving to a less expensive home.

Many home buyers are spending more on their smaller home and stepping up the level of luxury. This opens new possibilities for couples, singles, or single parents, as well as families with children, to choose the right size for their nests.

Does Moving Up Make Sense?

Answer these questions to help you decide whether moving up makes sense.

1. How much equity do you have in your home? Look at your annual mortgage statement or call your lender to find out. Usually, you don't build up much equity in the first few years of paying a mortgage, but if you've owned your home for a number of years, you may have significant unrealized gains.

2. Has your income increased enough to cover the extra mortgage costs and the costs of moving?

3. Does your neighborhood still meet your needs? For example, if you've had children, the quality of the schools may be more of a concern now than when you first purchased.

4. Can you add on or remodel? If you have a large yard, there might be room to expand your home. If not, your options may be limited. Also, do you want to undertake the headaches of remodeling?

5. How is the home market? If it's good, you may get top dollar for your home.

6. How are interest rates? A low rate not only helps you buy more home, but also makes it easier to find a buyer.

(Copyright 2006. Reprinted with permission from REALTOR® Magazine Online.)

Selling Under Pressure

If some life event is causing you to move before you had planned to, you might be in a position where you don't have enough equity (the amount of your home that you own after the outstanding mortgages or liens are paid off) in the home to sell. One of the best ways you can find out what your position truly is and what can be done about it is to talk with a professional real estate agent.

Your agent will help you go through your cash and loan position to see if you have enough equity to sell and explain some other possibilities to you, such as renting your home at a profit. Many real estate professionals are trained in specific areas of expertise, such as how to keep your home out of foreclosure, working with investors, or as property managers for rentals. When you hire your agent, as suggested in Chapter 2, you can find out if your agent has one or more of these areas of expertise.

The longer you've owned your home, the more likely it is that you can sell at a profit, but it is also just as likely that you might not be able to find another place as affordable as what you presently own.

Whatever the case may be, it's important to understand both your emotional and financial motivations before deciding to sell your home.

CHAPTER 2

Hiring an Agent to Help You Sell Your Home

Choosing the right real estate agent is as important as choosing an attorney, financial planner, or any other trusted adviser/consultant. For the goal of buying or selling a home, your agent is a partner who wants the same things you do: for you to sell your home at the best price and terms for your market, and to help the transaction go as smoothly as possible.

Experience plays an important role, as a veteran agent has been through all kinds of housing markets and knows the best strategies to help you sell your home, but the enthusiasm of a newer real estate professional can't be discounted. Both veteran and new real estate agents have the support of their brokers, who will also pitch in to help you reach your selling goals. The important thing is that you get the kind of service and support that's right for you.

You can always contact the agent who helped you buy your home. The agent's familiarity with the neighborhood and your particular home should be a plus, but what if you didn't have an agent for some reason? You might have purchased your home directly from the builder or another seller, or have inherited a family home. If so, you may be selling a home for the first time and wondering about the best way to go about finding the right real estate agent to help you market your property.

One direction that you could go is to ask for referrals from people you know who have recently sold homes in your area or nearby. Were they happy with their agent? Did the agent communicate well? How close did they come to getting the asking price? How long did it take? Would they hire the agent again?

Or you could shop listings in your own neighborhood. Attend open houses and see how the agents present themselves and the home they've listed. Check the homes online at REALTOR.com and see what kind of information is made available. Has the agent provided multiple photos or a virtual tour or video of the home? How much detail is there about the home, neighborhood, and schools, and is the information accurate?

Along with your title insurer, attorney, and others associated with the transaction, your real estate agent is part of your sales team. Your agent will help you identify trouble spots that could hinder the sale of your home and help you find the sources to fix problems and improve its marketability. Generally speaking, the team's job is to get you past the many obstacles that may come up between the time you decide to sell and when you close your deal.

The Difference between a REALTOR® and an Agent

All real estate agents are licensed by their states, but only REALTORS® are members of the NATIONAL ASSOCIATION OF REALTORS®. These professionals agree to abide by a higher standard of practice known as the REALTOR® Code of Ethics. In addition, they undergo continuing education and many pursue certifications and designations that distinguish their practices and enhance their experience.

According to the consumer section of NAR's web site (www.realtor.org/home_buyers_and_sellers/index.html), "Agents who represent buyers or sellers owe their clients a duty to place their client's interests first. In many states, agents are required by law to provide consumers with information setting forth their terms before embarking on a transaction."

Here are eight reasons to hire a real estate licensee to help you find a home and negotiate your transaction to a successful closing.

1. *Real estate professionals are market specialists.* No matter where you live, your housing market favors either sellers or buyers. Your agent will help you prepare your home to sell for the highest possible amount and educate you about the current market conditions. If you are looking for another home, your agent will help you with your new home.

2. *Real estate professionals are neighborhood experts.* While they are licensed to sell and manage real estate anywhere in the state, most real estate professionals wisely limit themselves to certain neighborhoods or types of homes such as new homes or condominiums. If you've never sold a home before, your agent can help you understand the selling process, including your responsibilities and those of the buyer.

3. *Real estate professionals have more information about homes than you do.* While it's fun to drive through neighborhoods and pop into open houses to see what your home may be competing against, you may not realize there is a vast amount of information about homes that may not be available to you unless you are working with your own agent. For example, some homes are sold without ever going into the local multiple listing service (MLS). If you don't know about them, how can you use them to help you determine the asking price of your home?

4. *Real estate professionals save you time.* If you want to sell your home quickly, put an agent to work for you. Over 85 percent of homes for sale in the United States are represented by agents. An agent acting as your listing agent (an agent who takes information about your home, packages it as a "listing" for their brokerage, and also enters it into the MLS and in advertising media to home buyers) is committed to getting you the best price and terms possible.

5. *Real estate professionals can work with you the way you want to work.* If you were in court, you'd want a good attorney by your side. As a seller, you also want an advocate. You can hire an agent as your exclusive fiduciary, which means he or she can't represent the buyer at the same time. Or you can hire a transactional broker who can handle both sides of the transaction without fiduciary preference to either side. While these agents are frequently paid on the back end of the transaction at closing, you can also hire an agent to perform certain tasks for an up-front fee, such as creating a comparable analysis for you, helping you with negotiations, or helping you find your next home.

6. *Real estate professionals share your risk.* With an agent by your side, you'll be less likely to make uninformed decisions because you'll know what issues you should consider carefully and why. All houses are imperfect, but some are more imperfect than others. While real estate agents don't take the place of home inspectors or contrac-

tors, they can certainly tell you what it will take to bring your home up to the market's standards and to help you with your disclosures to the buyer.

7. *Real estate professionals work to protect you from unqualified buyers.* While some buyers try to buy homes beyond their means, lenders and buyers' agents work to make sure that buyers know what they can afford and what range of homes they should be considering.

8. *Real estate professionals know how to close a deal.* Putting a home into the local MLS is the easy part. Getting the transaction to closing is the challenge, as so many factors can derail a home's sale, from market conditions to problems buyers may have in qualifying for your home due to rising interest rates, or problems selling their home so they can buy yours. Homeowner's insurance companies that withdraw from certain markets due to mold or damage from natural disasters cut new buyers off without warning (as recently happened in California and Texas). Inspection reports may reveal big problems you didn't know you had with your home. An agent will know exactly whom to call and what to do to solve any issue that threatens to keep the sale from moving toward closing.

Buyers and sellers share the same ultimate goal but have different priorities for achieving it. You want the most money and the best terms, while the buyer wants your home for the least amount of money and the best terms. It takes a skilled negotiator to keep the transaction moving forward.

Yes, you can sell your home on your own, but the rewards of working with an agent can be so much greater. Consider this: Selling a home has numerous steps associated with lots of time-consuming tasks along the way, not the least of which is learning about the market to present your home in the best light.

If you work a full-time job, when would you have time to market to buyers? To meet and qualify buyers? To show your home? To handle negotiations without getting emotional? Do you want strangers in your home who aren't represented by real estate agents? Having your home listed by a professional provides an important gateway that can lock out unwanted people from your home while welcoming qualified, motivated buyers. Hire a real estate agent, and save your energy for moving day.

Licensing Categories, Designations, and Certifications

In most states, with Colorado as a notable exception, there are two types of real estate licensees:

1. *Broker.* A broker has the highest level of real estate licensing. She can operate a brokerage and supervise salespeople who are also licensed by the state. Brokers can be managing brokers, which means the broker in charge, or they can serve as associate brokers with no company management duties. Salespeople report to the managing bro-

ker and do business according to the broker's business model. When you sign a listing agreement, you are contracting with the managing broker or with the firm itself (in some states, firms are licensed), even though you may be working with the broker's agent—a salesperson or associate broker.

2. *Salesperson.* A real estate salesperson is licensed to sell and manage real estate but acts as an agent of the broker. Your representation contract is actually with the broker, with your salesperson acting as the broker's agent.

Real estate agents also come in various stages of experience from newly licensed to seasoned veterans. To maintain their licenses, most real estate professionals are required to take continuing education courses to keep up with the changes in the law, state regulations, and local market rules.

Just as other professionals pursue higher education to hone their skills, real estate agents can do the same by becoming members and meeting the educational and business practice requirements of higher-level real estate organizations, particularly associations and nonprofit organizations that serve the real estate industry.

The real estate industry has been quick to meet the needs of sellers and buyers through professional development of its licensees. What these specially earned designations and certifications mean to you is that your agent has achieved a higher level of expertise in a given niche—the Internet, serving seniors, relocation, buyer's representation, and much more. That's not to say that certification-bearing agents can only help you in that particular niche, but it does mean they have more education and experience in that area.

Agents who go to the extra effort of putting in the time and expense to acquire designations and certifications not only are showing special interest in their business, but are demonstrating a desire to achieve a higher expertise in their profession. That is not to say that you wouldn't be as well served by someone who is new to the field or by a veteran who doesn't have extra credentials, but the chances are greater that a greater degree of knowledge in a particular specialty will be demonstrated by someone who has gone the extra mile.

Members of NAR affiliate organizations and real estate industry trade organizations are able to bring to each other networking skills that are invaluable to consumers. With a quick e-mail, an Accredited Buyer Representative (ABR) can contact a Certified Residential Specialist (CRS) about a listing to get more information. Both agents know that they are dealing with a professional at a higher level, even if they've never met.

The following list outlines the NAR-affiliated designations and certifications that may be helpful to you as a home seller.

- ABR: The Accredited Buyer Representative designation indicates a real estate agent specializing in representing buyers in the real estate transaction. The ABR is conferred by the Real Estate Buyer's Agent Council (REBAC).

- ABRM: The Accredited Buyer Representative Manager, also conferred by REBAC, is designed for those who manage or supervise buyer agents. Holding an ABR designation is a prerequisite for the ABRM, as is the supervision of 25 buyer representation transactions.

- At Home with Diversity: REALTORS® with the At Home with Diversity certification have been trained in and are sensitive to a wide range of cultural issues.

- CRB: The Certified Real Estate Brokerage Manager designation, conferred by the Real Estate Brokerage Managers Council, identifies brokers who have taken an extensive array of courses oriented toward enhancement of brokerage management skills.

- CRS: The Certified Residential Specialist designation by the Council of Residential Specialists denotes an agent who specializes in residential real estate. About 9 percent of the members of NAR have earned this designation.

- GRI: Approximately 18 percent of all REALTORS® have earned the designation Graduate REALTOR® Institute. The GRI designation identifies REALTORS® who are highly trained in many areas of real estate to better serve and protect their clients.

- RAA: The Residential Accredited Appraiser designation is for certified residential appraisers whose education and experience exceed state appraisal certification requirements.

- e-PRO®: The e-PRO® certification identifies real estate professionals who are trained in online marketing and communication technologies, and its graduates are considered to have a greater deal of Internet savvy.

- RSPS: The Resort and Second Home Property Specialist certification is for REALTORS® who specialize in the marketing, selling, and management of properties for investment, development, retirement, or second homes as a resort, recreational, and/or vacation destination.

As you can see, many of the NAR designations and certifications, conferred by its institutes, societies, and councils, approach almost graduate levels in terms of training. For more information on the NAR family of designations and certifications, please go to www.REALTOR.org and select the "Education" link.

In addition, there are other designations that are not affiliated with NAR but are held by numerous real estate agents.

- SRES: A Senior Real Estate Specialist specializes in senior issues, including financial planning as regards real estate.

- EBA: An Exclusive Buyer Agent works exclusively with buyers and never represents sellers or participates in dual agency.

- CRP: A Relocation Specialist is a specialist in the relocation process, including family issues, tax and legal issues, appraisals, and corporate relocation policies and issues.

Why Hire a Listing Agent?

A listing agent works for, and owes fiduciary responsibilities to, the real estate seller but keeps buyers' interests in mind throughout the marketing process for the home so your home is presented to other brokers, agents, and their buyers to its best advantage.

A listing agent will:

- Evaluate the market for pricing trends by comparing homes for sale and those that have recently sold.
- Assist you with strategies that help your home compete in its price range and locale.
- Keep abreast of changes in the marketplace that can impact the marketing of your home by previewing new listings on the market, evaluating feedback from showings of your home, and staying in constant communication with you so you know what's happening and why.
- Suggest other service providers who may be able to assist you with the presentation of your home, from landscapers to make-ready carpenters to stagers—people who come in to rearrange your belongings or help you clear out clutter to make your home more appealing.
- Present any offers to you and help you negotiate price and terms by keeping your best interests in mind.
- Most importantly, fully represent you throughout the real estate transaction.

Are You Thinking of Selling Your Home as a FSBO?

Since 1997, sellers who sell their home for-sale-by-owner (FSBO) have been trending downward. Only 13 percent of sellers in 2005 conducted transactions without the assistance of a real estate professional. Of those transactions, 39 percent were "closely held," which means they took place between sellers and buyers who knew each other, and the homes were never marketed to the general public.

The term FSBO can then be said to be something of a misnomer. If two out of five FSBO transactions are between related parties, and the homes are never placed on the open market, then a better term might be *unrepresented seller*.

The main reason that most sellers choose to hire a real estate professional is in the numbers; in 2005, the median home price for sellers with their own agent was 16 percent higher than homes sold directly by the owner. That's $230,000 versus $198,200.

Hiring Your Agent

If you are not sure how to go about hiring an agent, here are some recommendations:

Interview a Minimum of Three Agents

According to NAR research, most sellers choose the first agent they meet or the first agent who is recommended to them, so make

Questions to Ask When Choosing an Agent

1. How long have you been in residential real estate sales? Is this your full-time job? (While experience is no guarantee of skill, real estate, like many other professions, is mostly learned on the job.)

2. What designations do you hold? (Designations such as GRI and CRS, which require that real estate professionals take additional, specialized real estate training, are held by only about a quarter of real estate practitioners.)

3. How many homes did you and your company sell last year?

4. How many days did it take you to sell the average home? How did that compare to the overall market?

5. How close to the initial asking prices of the homes you sold were the final sale prices?

6. What types of specific marketing systems and approaches will you use to sell my home? (Look for someone who has aggressive, innovative approaches, not just someone who's going to put a sign in the yard and hope for the best.)

7. Will you represent me exclusively, or will you represent both the buyer and the seller in the transaction? (While it's usually legal to represent both parties in a transaction, it's important to understand where the practitioner's obligations lie. A good practitioner will explain the agency relationship to you and describe the rights of each party. It's also possible to request that the practitioner represent you exclusively.)

(Continued)

Questions to Ask When Choosing an Agent (Continued)

8. Can you recommend service providers who can assist me in obtaining a mortgage, making repairs on my home, and other things I need done? (Keep in mind here that real estate professionals should generally recommend more than one provider and should tell you if they receive any compensation from any provider.)

9. What type of support and supervision does your brokerage office provide to you? (Having resources, such as in-house support staff, access to a real estate attorney, or assistance with technology, can help a real estate professional sell your home.)

10. What's your business philosophy? (While there's no right answer to this question, the response will help you assess what's important to the real estate practitioner—fast sales, service, and so on—and determine how closely the practitioner's goals and business emphasis mesh with your own.)

11. How will you keep me informed about the progress of my transaction? How frequently? Using what media? (Again, this is not a question with a correct answer, but one that reflects your desires. Do you want updates twice a week or don't want to be bothered unless there's a hot prospect? Do you prefer phone, e-mail, or a personal visit?)

12. Could you please give me the names and phone numbers of your three most recent clients?

(Copyright 2006. Reprinted with permission from REALTOR® Magazine Online.)

sure that person is in tune with your experience level and is someone who has resources to help you sell your home with lots of support from his or her company to make your transaction go as smoothly as possible. Possible sources to find the right agent are:

- Asking family and friends for referrals.
- Meeting agents at open houses and other events.
- Meeting agents online or through other advertising.

You may find you already know an agent who is also a friend or family member. While it may seem like a great idea to hire this person, remember that your personal relationship stands the chance of being affected by the businesslike negotiations of selling your home.

Look for Professionalism

Agents can work full- or part-time, but you want a professional, someone who is up to date in the market, has the latest education or continuing education, and takes her responsibilities seriously enough to be available full-time. There are too many changes in the law, the local market, and mortgage loans to risk your most important transaction on someone who isn't committed to you.

You also want someone who is continually updating his own skills as well as his education. While some continuing education may be required for licensure, find out if the agent has gone beyond the minimum requirement to seek out other certifications or designations. Be sure to ask what is the latest skill the agent has added to his toolbox. Has he recently taken a technology course? Attended a class on architecture? The answer might be very revealing.

Evaluate the Answers According to Your Needs

While you want an agent who is compatible with you and your family, other attributes may be just as important, if not more so. Your agent should:

- *Be knowledgeable.* Your agent should know the benefits and challenges of selling homes in your neighborhood. For example, a condominium community offers a different lifestyle and homeowner responsibilities from single-family home ownership. If you are selling a property of this nature, this should be carefully explained to potential buyers, especially if they have never owned a home in a community operated by a homeowners association (HOA), management company, hotel, or other third-party management.

- *Be a good educator.* Your agent should be able to explain what you need to know to sell your home, so you make the fewest mistakes possible and get as close to meeting your goals as possible. If you are using the same agent to help you move to a new home, he or she should show you housing inventory within your qualifying range.

- *Be capable.* Your agent should be able to meet your special needs as a seller, such as time constraints. First-time sellers may have more need for assistance and attention than experienced sellers and may not understand that some markets are more sluggish than others. An experienced agent knows which strategies work best no matter what the market conditions.

■ *Be a good communicator.* Your agent should keep you informed of the latest listings, interest rate alerts, market conditions, and other data that could impact your transaction. Frequent communication by e-mail, phone, or fax is desirable.

■ *Be experienced.* Experience is relative. One agent may have years of experience in selling real estate but not in your neighborhood. A new agent, on the other hand, may not have much experience in sales, but she may bowl you over with enthusiasm and energy, or he may have the Internet communication skills to market your home. Judge an agent's experience on how you prefer they work with you.

Choose the Best Candidate

By the time you interview at least three agents, you'll have a better idea of which agent is most likely to meet your needs. If you don't feel comfortable, keep looking!

To have a good working relationship, be as honest as you can about your needs, wants, and abilities. Be flexible in allowing your agent to show you ideas you haven't thought about. Moving that chair might really make the room look larger. Taking down your family pictures may really help buyers envision themselves in your home. Give the agent the chance to make things right when they don't go according to plan.

Understanding Representation

It's important to understand what legal responsibilities your real estate salesperson has to you and to other parties in the transaction. Ask your salesperson to explain what type of agency relationships are available to you if you elect to work with him or her and with the brokerage company.

1. *Seller's representative* (also known as a *listing agent* or *seller's agent*). A seller's agent is hired by and represents the seller. All fiduciary duties are owed to the seller. The agency relationship usually is created by a listing contract.

2. *Subagent.* A subagent owes the same fiduciary duties to the agent's principal as the agent does. Subagency usually arises when a cooperating sales associate from another brokerage, who is not representing the buyer as a buyer's representative or operating in a nonagency relationship, shows property to a buyer. In such a case, the subagent works with the buyer as a customer but owes fiduciary duties to the listing broker and the seller. Although a subagent cannot assist the buyer in any way that would be detrimental to the seller, a buyer–customer can expect to be treated honestly by the subagent. It is important that subagents fully explain their duties to buyers.

3. *Buyer's representative* (also known as a *buyer's agent*). A real estate licensee who is hired by prospective buyers to represent them in a real estate transaction. The buyer's rep works in the buyer's best interest throughout the transac-

tion and owes fiduciary duties to the buyer. The buyer can pay the licensee directly through a negotiated fee, or the buyer's rep may be paid by the seller or by a commission split with the listing broker.

4. *Disclosed dual agent.* Dual agency is a relationship in which the brokerage firm represents both the buyer and the seller in the same real estate transaction. Dual agency relationships do not carry with them all of the traditional fiduciary duties to the clients. Instead, dual agents owe limited fiduciary duties. Because of the potential for conflicts of interest in a dual agency relationship, it's vital that all parties give their informed consent. In many states, this consent must be in writing. Disclosed dual agency, in which both the buyer and the seller are told that the agent is representing both of them and both consent to such an arrangement, is legal in most states.

5. *Designated agent* (also called, among other things, *appointed agency*). This is a brokerage practice that allows the managing broker to designate which licensees in the brokerage will act as an agent of the seller and which will act as an agent of the buyer. Designated agency avoids the problem of creating a dual agency relationship for licensees at the brokerage. The designated agents give their clients full representation, with all of the attendant fiduciary duties. The broker still has the responsibility of supervising both groups of licensees.

6. *Nonagency relationship* (called, among other things, a *transaction broker* or *facilitator*). Some states permit a real estate

licensee to have a type of nonagency relationship with a consumer. These relationships vary considerably from state to state, both as to the duties owed to the consumer and the name used to describe them. Very generally, the duties owed to the consumer in a nonagency relationship are less than the complete, traditional fiduciary duties of an agency relationship.

(Copyright 2006. Reprinted with permission from REALTOR® Magazine Online.)

Agency Disclosure

Most states require real estate agents to disclose to consumers if they have a relationship with the other party in a potential transaction. For example, your listing agent may represent you in a fiduciary manner, which means he won't share any information with other parties that could result in a lower price for your home. But he may meet a potential buyer while holding an open house for your property. At that time, your listing agent may need to disclose his relationship as your listing agent to the buyer. The buyer may still wish to work with your agent, but the buyer will be a customer of your agent while you remain the client.

The Listing Presentation and Agreement

When you sign a listing agreement, you are contracting with the brokerage company or the managing broker of the company to sell your home. The listing agent, who serves as the agent of the brokerage, is your contact at the brokerage as well as your representative.

The listing agreement should spell out the responsibilities and activities of your broker, the broker's agent, as well as their compensation (commission or fee-for-service) and the length of time or term of the contract.

It is the written listing contract that authorizes a broker to market a seller's home. This agreement typically also authorizes the broker to enter the home into the local MLS.

Six Items Usually Included in Listing Presentations

1. A comparable market analysis, along with the agent's personal analysis of your property.

2. The agent's bio and information about the brokerage he or she represents.

3. A detailed marketing plan for the home.

4. An explanation of the services the agent will provide for his/her compensation.

5. An agency disclosure form.

6. A listing agreement, ready to be signed except for the price and the terms.

(Copyright 2006. Reprinted with permission from REALTOR® Magazine Online.)

The MLS is a business-to-business cooperative among participating brokers for the sole purpose of making their listings available to other brokers and their agents to sell and to offer compensation for that cooperation. It's more like a storeroom, rather than a showroom.

Multiple listing services operate with rules in order to treat all brokers the same way. They have guidelines for the submission of listings, for changing information such as price, and using the listing in advertising. When a listing agent lists a home, the MLS information includes basics about the property including price, estimated square footage or approximate room size, number of bedrooms and baths, special features, tax information, showing instructions, and much more. It also includes the offer of compensation to the selling broker whose agent brings the successful buyer.

It is in sellers' best interest to have their homes in the local MLS because most listed homes are sold through agent cooperation, but keep in mind that putting a home into the MLS doesn't necessarily get the home in front of the public. The MLS is for brokers, not an advertising medium for consumers. Most MLSs don't have a public Internet site, and others don't allow their database of listings to be published on the Internet on public sites. Some MLSs may charge consumers for the opportunity to view information about the listings.

That said, many homes for sale are available for viewing online, and consumers are aware of this fact. The Internet has quickly become the most popular way for buyers to search for homes. The *2005 NAR Profile of Home Buyers and Sellers* found that:

- Overall, 57 percent of all home buyers use the Internet to search for a home.

- 82 percent of first-time home buyers use the Internet to search for a home.

- From 1997 to 2005, the percentage of home buyers who first found the home they purchased on the Internet has increased from 2 percent to 24 percent.

Most REALTOR®-listed homes are advertised on REALTOR.com, where listing brokers can enhance the listing for the public by including multiple photos of the property, neighborhood information, mortgage information, virtual tours, and much more. However, not all information is included to ensure a client's confidentiality.

In addition, your agent may have a number of other means to market your listing, according to what she feels is effective for your market, price range, type of home, and your motivation to sell. These include open houses, broker luncheons, magazine and newspaper advertisements, web site ads, television ads, and more.

Listings are the foundation of real estate sales, as it is listings that create inventory to show to buyers. Listing agents do quite a bit of work in advance of the listing appointment in order to secure the listing, including mailing or delivering prelisting packages that illustrate how their company and their marketing expertise is best for you and your home.

The listing broker enters the listing information into the MLS with an offer of cooperation to selling brokers (buyer's brokers) to help her get the listing sold. The listing broker also specifies the amount of compensation to be paid to the selling broker.

Negotiating Commissions

Your broker knows what it takes to stay in business as well as to help your home compete in the market. Many have a firm policy about commissions, and your salesperson or associate broker may not be authorized to negotiate commissions that deviate from company policy.

The main reason is the risk factor. Commissions are typically paid at the close of the transaction. If the house doesn't sell, the agent and broker get nothing and are out the marketing time, effort, and all direct and indirect expenses.

While service levels certainly vary, real estate agents provide a long list of services to successfully market a home, including:

- Present your home to its best advantage from staging the home (see more about this in Chapter 4) to fixing problems that will affect your pricing.
- Price your home by using a detailed market analysis of comparable properties recently sold and by comparing those that are currently on the market.
- List your property in the local MLS as well as advertising sites designed for the public.
- Put a sign in your yard to attract neighborhood drivers.
- Create a feature sheet that is available for buyers to take from open houses, yard sign tubes, and other special events.

- Research the best means for targeted buyers to purchase your home with appropriate financing options.

- Schedule tours of your home for other agents.

- Create JUST LISTED fliers or mailers to be distributed to neighbors and in nearby move-up and rental neighborhoods.

- Advertise in publications that will attract buyers to your area and price range, including newspapers, home magazines, and the Internet.

- Schedule open houses and other events to stimulate activity.

- Keep you informed of current market conditions by providing feedback on showings, copies of all ads regarding your home, and keeping you abreast of any changes in the marketplace including new competition on the market.

- Review your property's market placement after 30 days if it hasn't sold, and make recommendations on what to do to sell it.

- Put only qualified buyers into consideration for your home by ensuring they are prequalified with lenders and screening buyers by answering questions about your home.

- Sell buyers on taking action by offering the most information about the neighborhood and competing properties and your home's features.

- Negotiate the purchase agreement and, in doing so, represent your best interests as your listing agent.

- Coordinate all of the closing details:

  Follow up with buyer's mortgage application.

  Schedule appraisal.

  Provide appraiser with comparable sales.

  Order all title work.

  Order lender(s) payoff.

  Coordinate all inspections, including termite, gas, radon, well, septic, property inspection, and other certifications (if necessary).

  Review the settlement figures for accuracy.

  Arrange for power of attorney (if needed).

- Be on hand to handle last-minute contingencies concerning the contract, inspection, appraisal, or anything else not completed before closing.

- Accompany you to closing and help you through the settlement procedure.

- Stay in regular contact to make sure everything is in order.

(List adapted from *Realty Times* archives, by DeLena Ciamacco.)

Commissions are negotiable and may vary, but so do service levels. The best way you can tell if you are going to get your money's worth is to make sure you understand what services you are buying.

If you intend to ask a professional to cut his fees, think carefully about whether that's truly in your best interest. You're paying a commission to ensure promptness, loyalty, and hard work. While your salesperson may gracefully accept a lower fee, you may find that the agent must cut back on some service in order to make your deal work.

Be clear about what you expect, what you are paying for, and how you measure what you are getting.

Ask for a detailed marketing plan to make sure you and your agent are on the same page. A detailed marketing plan should contain the following:

- A marketing period for your home.
- A calendar of events, which may include agent tours and open houses.
- Ad placements and results.
- A guideline for communication—once a week e-mail or phone calls, for example.
- A feedback mechanism to get comments from agents and home buyers.
- A date to reassess the marketing plan and make revisions if necessary.

Some brokers have adjusted their business models to be able to provide à la carte service to sellers. You can negotiate with the broker for certain services while not paying for other services you think you don't want. In those situations, you won't pay on the back end because there's no reward to the listing agent for selling the home. Be prepared to pay for fee-for-service brokerage services at the time services are delivered.

Some sellers may not be in a position to pay much commission because they've been transferred and haven't had time to build much equity, or their home needs quite a bit of updates and they don't have the cash.

Sit down with your agent and go over the financials regarding your home. You may be surprised at how empathetic your agent can be. She may be able to come up with a creative solution for you.

Types of Listing Agreements

There are different kinds of listing contracts, the most popular of which is the *exclusive right to sell,* which means the broker has the exclusive right to market your home to other real estate professionals and consumers. Another important feature of an exclusive right to sell listing agreement is that the broker is entitled to compensation if the home sells during the term of the agreement regardless of who found the buyer. This is typical of the full-service listing.

In some markets, brokers have agreements with sellers to both list and sell the home without providing a cooperative fee to other brokers to bring buyers. This is usually a form of discounting to the seller in which they pay the broker less but the broker is able to work both sides of the transaction in a nonagency form of representation so they can also represent the buyer.

Limited service listings are actually a level of service provided in exclusive listing agreements. They typically include entry of the listing into the MLS and whatever services you agree upon with the broker. This means that you are paying the broker for a limited menu of services, in an à la carte fashion. You might pay the broker, for example, to list your home in the MLS for a fee that is usually paid up front and is nonrefundable. You might also pay extra for a yard sign.

Essentially the listing agreement is about risk—the risk that your home will sell to a qualified buyer—and the fees you pay a broker relate to that risk. The more the broker does for you, the higher the fee may be to the broker. The less the broker does for you, the lower the fee may be to the broker.

To save money, you might choose to show your home or do your own negotiating with no input from the broker.

The Value of the Comparable Market Analysis

Your broker will provide you a comparable market analysis (CMA) of your home that will show its position in the current market. The CMA is used to lay the groundwork for setting a realistic selling price for the property. The analysis should include:

- All active, comparable properties in the neighborhood.

- All comparable properties that have sold within the past six months.

- All comparable listings in the neighborhood that have expired (i.e., not sold by the end date of their original listing agreement) within the past six months.

- A summary of the pricing trends in the local real estate market over the past year.

- A summary of the average number of days on the market for comparable homes within the past year.

- Any available third-party data (as provided by the local board of REALTORS®) on market trends in your area.

It's important to remember that a CMA is useful for only a brief period, and should not be the only tool used to help you set a price for your home or to help you choose an agent.

CMAs reflect the most current market information and can include comparable homes within a few streets, blocks, or an entire ZIP code. The more like-style homes that are present in the CMA, the more accurate yours is likely to be.

Keep in mind that every home is unique because of its location, condition, and features. Your home may compare favorably to other homes based on the care you've given it. Homes that are well-maintained and updated with fresh paint, landscaping, new appliances, or other amenities are the most likely to sell for the highest price in any market.

You can find comparables from Internet sites, many of which use automated home valuations as a means to lead you to real estate agents. However, these online calculations aren't always accurate or are from data sources that are out of date. Your agent may know why one comparable home sold for more or less than another because she's been inside both houses. Real estate professionals know which houses were updated, which weren't, which have floor plan or location problems, and so on. Automated online home valuation tools have no way of accessing this type of hands-on information.

For the latest and most accurate information, use CMAs provided by your agent. As your home enters the market, your agent should supply you with ongoing updates as to the status of the marketplace so you can adjust your marketing accordingly.

CHAPTER 3

Preparing and Pricing Your Home to Sell

More than seven million existing homes were sold in 2005, and while each transaction is different, every owner wants the same thing—the best possible deal with the least amount of problems.

Preventing problems with the sale is one of the best strategies for selling your home, and that can easily be done by preparing your home properly for the market.

Unfortunately, home selling has become a more complex business than it used to be. New seller disclosure statements, longer and more detailed form agreements, and a range of environmental concerns have all emerged in the past decade.

More importantly, the home-selling process has changed. Buyer brokerage—where real estate agents represent home buyers—is now common nationwide, and good buyer–brokers want the best for their clients, too.

The result is that while almost 100,000 existing homes are sold each week, the process is not as easy for sellers as it was 5 or 10 years ago.

Are You Ready?

The home-selling process typically starts several months before a property is made available for sale. It's necessary to look at a home through the eyes of a prospective buyer and determine what needs to be cleaned, painted, repaired, and tossed out.

Ask yourself: If you were buying this home, what would you want to see? The goal is to show a home that looks attractive, maximizes space, and appeals to as many buyers as possible.

While part of the getting ready phase relates to repairs, painting, and other home improvements, this is also a good time to ask why you really want to sell.

Selling a home is an important matter and there should be a good reason to sell—perhaps a job change to a new community or the need for more space. Your reason for selling can impact the negotiating process, so it's important to discuss your needs and wants in private with the agent who lists your home.

When Should You Sell?

The marketplace tends to be more active in the spring and early summer because parents want to enroll children in classes at the beginning of the school year (usually August). Spring and summer are also typically when most homes are likely to be available.

Generally speaking, markets tend to have some balance between buyers and sellers year-round. In a given community, for example, there may be fewer buyers in late December, but there are also likely to be fewer homes available for purchase. So home prices tend to rise or fall because of general demand patterns rather than the time of the year.

Keeping that in mind, owners are encouraged to sell when the property is ready for sale, there is a need or desire to sell, and the services of a local agent have been retained.

How Do You Improve Your Home's Value?

The general rule in real estate is that buyers seek the least expensive home in the best neighborhood they can afford. In terms of improvements, this means your home should fit in the neighborhood but should not be overimproved. For example, if most homes in your neighborhood have three bedrooms, two baths, and

2,500 square feet of finished space, a property with five bedrooms, more baths, and far more space would likely be priced much higher and be more difficult to sell.

Improvements should be made so that the property shows well, is consistent with the neighborhood, and does not involve capital investments, which may not be recovered from the sale. Furthermore, improvements should reflect community preferences.

Cosmetic improvements—paint, wallpaper, and landscaping—help a home show better and often are good investments. Mechanical repairs—to ensure that all systems and appliances are in good working condition—are required to get a top price.

Ideally, you want to be sure that your property is competitive with other homes available in the community. Real estate agents see numerous homes and can provide suggestions that are consistent with your marketplace.

However, if you need major improvements, you should consider your return on investment versus how much the improvements will increase the sales price of your home. If you are in doubt, talk to your real estate agent about the following projects for your home:

Repairs That Matter the Most

It goes without saying that cosmetic touch-ups are appealing, but buyers are also strongly influenced by the operating condition of the electrical and plumbing systems, air-conditioning and heating systems, and major appliances. They want to know that the roof and gutters are good for at least several more years if not longer. Windows and doors with good seals and insulation in the attic are also important for keeping drafts away and operating costs down.

Repairs are one of the few ways the buyer has to judge the honesty of the seller and the integrity of the home. If small items for repair have been overlooked or ignored, the buyer will assume that larger, more important items have also been neglected.

This is one area where a homeowner's inspection and your agent's make-ready team could come in handy. The inspection will tell you the trouble spots, and either you or your agent can address the problems with a short list of carpenters, plumbers, electricians, handypersons, and/or contractors.

The idea is to pay close attention to any fixture that unchecked could cause you greater expense—leaks that could raise water bills, broken tiles that could cause falls, wood damage or rot that could invite insect infestations, and so on.

Remodeling Costs

While most agents aren't plumbers, electricians, or contractors, they should still be experienced enough to help sellers decide which remodeling projects are most worthwhile.

With that in mind, NAR partners with Hanley Wood LLC every year to do an extensive cost versus value report for *Remodeling* magazine. The report covers the costs, resale value, and percentage recouped at sale for 18 of the most popular remodeling projects. The most recent report includes some interesting data.

- A typical bathroom remodel costs $10,499 and can expect a return of $10,727 (102.2 percent return).

- A typical mid-range kitchen remodel costs $43,862 and can expect a return of $39,920 (91 percent return).

- A typical master bedroom suite costs $137,891, but returns only $110,512 on resale (80 percent return).

The report is interesting because homeowners spent more than $139 billion on home improvements and repairs in 2005, according to data from Harvard's Joint Center for Housing Studies.

Interestingly, the desirability of different remodeling projects varied greatly by region and metropolitan area. In the West, for example, window replacements are highly valued, perhaps due in part to insulation and cooling concerns in desert regions, with nearly 103 percent of costs recouped on sale. Westerners also prefer remodeled kitchens and basements; in this region, for example, a minor mid-range kitchen remodel may return 112.3 percent, and a basement remodel is estimated to return 108 percent.

In the Midwest, however, the same kitchen and basement projects return only 85 and 73 percent, respectively. Midwest buyers appreciate homes with updated siding; mid-range and upscale siding replacements return 96 and 98 percent of the project costs, respectively. Siding replacement projects fared well at resale in all four regions, likely because new siding is a relatively inexpensive way to update and refresh a home's curb appeal.

Buyers in the South are partial to upscale bathrooms, which return an average of 98.5 percent of project costs. When considering resale value, however, southerners may want to think twice about mid-range window replacements; this improvement, which is so popular in the West, only returns an average of 83.7 percent of project costs in the South.

In the East, a mid-range attic bedroom addition returns an average of 98.1 percent at resale, but a home office remodel returns only 75 percent. In fact, remodeling projects that involved home offices were among the lowest returns on investment across all four regions.

To view the complete report, visit REALTOR® Magazine Online (www.REALTOR.org/rmodaily.nsf) and click on the Cost vs. Value Report link under the Special Features section.

Finding a Good Remodeler

To learn more about remodeling, visit the National Association of the Remodeling Industry (NARI) at www.nari.org. You will learn about the importance of certification. NARI certifies its members based on their experience and dedication to quality and customer service. In order to become NARI-certified, a remodeler must be a full-time professional with at least five years experience. You will want to choose a remodeler with the most experience in the area of the home you want redone. A kitchen and bath specialist, for example, will be certified as a NARI CKBR. Be sure to check the certifications at www.nari.org.

Twelve Tips for Hiring a Remodeling Contractor

1. Get at least three written estimates.

2. Get references and call to check on the work. If possible, go by and visit earlier jobs.

3. Check with the local chamber of commerce or Better Business Bureau for complaints.

4. Be sure that the contract states exactly what is to be done and how change orders will be handled.

5. Make as small a down payment as possible so you won't lose a lot if the contractor fails to complete the job.

6. Be sure that the contractor has the necessary permits, licenses, and insurance.

7. Be sure that the contract states when the work will be completed and what recourse you have if it isn't. Also remember that in many instances you can cancel a contract within three business days of signing it.

8. Ask if the contractor's workers will do the entire job or whether subcontractors will do parts.

9. Get the contractor to indemnify you if work does not meet local building codes or regulations.

10. Be sure that the contract specifies the contractor will clean up after the job and be responsible for any damage.

11. Guarantee that materials used meet your specifications.

12. Don't make the final payment until you're satisfied with the work.

(Copyright 2006. Reprinted with permission from REALTOR® Magazine Online.)

First Impressions Count

Remember that many buyers' first impression of your home will be what they find on Internet sites such as REALTOR.com. Nearly four out of five buyers view homes online where they will look at photos, take virtual tours, and view videos of homes. Your agent will market your home according to your wishes, but keep in mind that your home needs to be camera-ready—clean, tasteful, and attractive.

Five Things to Do Before You Sell

1. Get estimates from a reliable repairperson on items that need to be replaced soon, such as a roof or worn carpeting, for example. In this way, buyers will have a better sense of how much these needed repairs will affect their costs.

2. Have a termite inspection to prove to buyers that the property is not infested.

3. Get a presale home inspection so you'll be able to make repairs before buyers become concerned and cancel a contract.

4. Gather together warranties and guarantees on the furnace, appliances, and other items that will remain with the house.

5. Fill out a disclosure form provided by your sales associate. Take the time to be sure that you don't forget to disclose problems, however minor, that might create liability for you after the sale.

(Copyright 2006. Reprinted with permission from REALTOR® Magazine Online.)

The Importance of Curb Appeal

Buyers also drive or walk through neighborhoods they are interested in. They may download information about your listing from the Internet and come to see if they are interested in your home. Or they may drive around looking for homes for sale on their favorite streets. Buyer's agents will also preview homes for their customers and may include your home for a showing (an appointment made between your listing agent and the buyer's agent to see your home at an appointed time).

If the buyer doesn't like the appeal of your home from the street, it's much harder for the buyer's agent to say, "Let's give it a chance and see what's on the inside."

To make certain your home shows well from the street, work on your curb appeal.

Interior Appeal

When buyers enter your home, you want them to feel welcome, but they should also be able to put themselves in your shoes as the next homeowner. The easier time they have picturing their family activities and placing their furniture, the better chance you have of making the sale.

Ten Ways to Improve Your Curb Appeal

1. Get rid of any clutter in the yard—children's toys, broken tree branches, bikes, unattractive lawn furniture.

2. Wash your windows and screens to let more light into the interior.

3. Clean out the garage and organize your storage. Park vehicles away from the home for showings.

4. Open drapes, shutters, and blinds to let in more light and make the home appear more inviting.

5. Make minor repairs to items that can create a bad impression. Small problems, such as sticky doors, torn screens, cracked caulking, or peeling paint give buyers the impression that the house isn't well-maintained.

6. Tidy your yard. Cut the grass, rake the leaves, trim the bushes, and edge the walks. Put a pot or two of bright flowers near the entryway. Replace dead or leggy bushes and plant flowers in your beds.

7. Patch holes in your driveway and reapply sealant, if applicable.

8. Clean your gutters.

9. Polish your front doorknob and door numbers. Put out a fresh, new welcome mat.

10. Paint trim, doors, and windows with fresh, updated color.

(Copyright 2006. Reprinted with permission from REALTOR® Magazine Online.)

Any real estate professional will tell you that the first thing you need to do is remove clutter. It's distracting to buyers and no matter how much space you have, it looks as if you don't have enough.

Start thinking of all your belongings and what you want to do with them. Decide what to keep, give away, or throw away.

Dividing your household goods into three simple categories (keep, give away, throw away) can make your life so much easier when you stage your home to sell. Be ruthless. If you haven't used an item in more than a year, donate it or throw it away. If you want to keep it, ask yourself if you want to pay by the pound to move it. See more about moving in Chapter 11.

To Have a Yard Sale or Not to Have a Yard Sale

In the middle of preparing your home to sell, conducting a yard sale may seem like more work and trouble than it's worth. In some ways, you're right. People often pay pennies on the dollar for items you once paid full retail for, and at the end of the day, you may come out only a few hundred dollars richer.

In addition, you have to advertise the sale and put signs all around the yard, price and sticker each item, and so on. (You also may not want to advertise that you are planning on selling your house.)

The day of the sale, people come knocking on your door before the sun is up, and you have to remain alert and vigilant all day to having strangers in your yard.

For other people, yard sales are a load of fun. Here are some suggestions on how to make a yard sale work for you.

Ten Tips for Holding a Yard Sale

Hold a yard sale to reduce the clutter in your home and get rid of items you don't want to move.

1. Check with your city government to see if you need a permit or license.

2. See if neighbors want to participate and have a block sale to attract more visitors.

3. Advertise. Put an ad in free classified papers, and put up signs and balloons at major intersections and in stores near your home.

4. Price items ahead and attach prices with removable stickers. Remember, yard sales are supposed to be bargains, so don't try to sell anything of significant value this way.

5. Check items before the sale to be sure you haven't included something you want by mistake.

6. Keep pets away from the sale.

7. Display everything neatly and individually so customers don't have to dig through boxes.

8. Have an electrical outlet so buyers can test appliances.

9. Have plenty of bags and newspaper for wrapping fragile items.

10. Get enough change, and keep a close eye on your cash.

A Word about Pets

According to the National Pet Owners Survey by the American Pet Products Manufacturers Association (APPMA), pet ownership is at the highest level in history. Nearly 63 percent of all U.S. households own a pet, which equates to about 69 million homes.

Pets are often so loved by their owners that they are allowed the run of the house. Unfortunately, that may mean that it's hard to realize how much these pets may be hurting your marketing efforts in selling your home if you are a pet lover. Some people are frightened of other people's pets, or they may be allergic to pet dander.

Here are seven things to keep in mind:

1. *If it smells, it won't sell.* Your pet may be perfectly well mannered, but that doesn't mean your home is odor free. Most pet odor comes from fur and dander. Pets mark their territory by rubbing their fur on objects. That's why your cat rubs your ankles with her sides. Minimize pet odors by not allowing your pets to sleep on couches and carpets. Provide them with a bed of their own and reward them lavishly whenever they use it. Keep pets bathed and groomed more often than usual, so as not to add to existing pet odor.

2. *Stains don't have to be permanent.* There are many good products to clean pet stains. Just visit your local pet store or key "pet stains" into your favorite search engine. Hospital supply companies are also a great source for stain and

odor control products. You can also pay a carpet expert to cut out stained patches and replace them with remnants.

3. *Vacuum daily*. While your home is being marketed, vacuum the carpets daily with a deodorizer. You can find one in the cleaning supplies section of the grocery store. Remember to change bags more frequently than usual. Treat your home to a professional carpet cleaning. Also open the windows and let some fresh air in. Pull back the drapes. Open vents. A closed-in home will hold more odor than it should.

4. *Keep pets from showings*. If buyers don't see a pet, there's a good chance they'll look at the home more objectively. If they spot your dog or cat, they will be alerted to look for stains and odors. Arrange to have your pet off the property for showings, and put their food dishes and toys out of sight, too.

5. *Stains and odors may have to be disclosed*. Check with your agent to see if your state requires disclosure of stains that haven't been removed. If you aren't sure what the extent of your pet's damage is, you can purchase, rent, or borrow a hand-held black light to shine on carpets and other fixtures. Some carpet cleaning kits include a black light for this purpose. Viewing your carpet this way will help you decide whether to clean or replace the carpet. Your agent will most likely advise you to replace the carpet or offer a carpet allowance to buyers. It will cost you much less money than a repulsed buyer's discount.

6. *Perception is everything*. If your home doesn't pass the sniff or stain test, it will adversely affect the way other agents and

their buyers perceive your home. Your agent is depending upon other agents to show your home to their buyers. Many agents insist on showing only pristine homes to their clients. Once word gets around, you may find yourself with few showings, which may cause the value of your home to drop.

7. *Be realistic about your home's value.* A home is really worth only what a buyer is willing to pay. If your home has suffered damage due to your pets, it may be devalued in the marketplace. The only cure is taking action to eliminate the problem before your home goes on the market. Listen to your agent and follow his advice about the most cost-effective ways to manage your pet's damage to the home. He will have suggestions and solutions that will put you right back on the marketing track.

Price It Right the First Time

Pricing your home to sell is one of your agent's greatest areas of expertise and an important reason why sellers benefit from professional assistance.

If you are working with an agent who is a specialist in your neighborhood, she will be more familiar than anyone else on what homes are selling for and how long it took for homes in your area to sell. This knowledge of market value is valuable for home sellers to get the best offers for their homes.

The closer your asking price is to market value, the faster it will sell. The trick is in determining whether the market is trending upward or downward. You want to price your home low enough to entice buyers but not so low that you leave money on the table.

You may be tempted to price your home to help you meet financial goals such as retirement or to pay for your child's college, but keep in mind that buyers will be considering the same comparables that you have. Also, if you've reduced the equity in your home by taking out loans to pay off credit cards instead of using them for home improvements, you may find it difficult to price your home competitively. It's important to understand what the market will bear, and a reputable agent will provide that expertise for you.

If you have made a recent improvement, it's tempting to try to recoup your costs. As you learned earlier in this chapter, some improvements add more value than others. It's really up to the buyer whether they see value in what you've done. For example, if you've put in a new countertop in the kitchen, and the buyer doesn't like your choice, she is thinking about paying you for something she doesn't like, plus the costs of tearout and replacement. That's why buyers tend to discount features they don't like so drastically. It's also a good reason why you shouldn't do major remodeling work if you are planning on selling your home.

Keep in mind that buyers may view the same amenity differently. Some consider a swimming pool to be the ultimate in summertime fun, while other buyers see only maintenance costs and safety issues.

While it takes a lot of discipline, you must be realistic in distinguishing between cost and value.

Tips on How to Price Your Home

- Consider comparables. What have other homes in your neighborhood sold for recently? How do they compare to yours in terms of size, upkeep, and amenities?

- Consider competition. How many other homes are for sale in your area? Are you competing against new homes?

- Consider your contingencies. Do you have special concerns that would affect the price you'll receive? For example, do you want to be able to move in four months?

- Get an appraisal. For a few hundred dollars, a qualified appraiser can give you an estimate of your home's value. Be sure to ask for a market-value appraisal. To locate appraisers in your area, contact the Appraisal Institute (www.AppraisalInstitute.org), or ask your agent for some recommendations.

- Be accurate. Studies show that homes priced higher than 3 percent over the correct price take longer to sell.

- Know what you'll accept. It's critical to know what price you'll accept before beginning a negotiation with a buyer.

(Copyright 2006. Reprinted with permission from REALTOR® Magazine Online.)

CHAPTER 4

Staging Your Home for Profit

What Is Staging?

When I decorate a house, I bring in plants, pictures, and with staging, I am taking out plants that are the wrong size or make rooms look smaller.

—Peggy Selinger-Eaton

You may have heard that you must spend thousands of dollars to "stage" a house. Not true! Staging, or enhancing the impression your home forms in the mind of the buyer, can consist of simple things you can do yourself, says staging expert Peggy Selinger-Eaton (www.peggyscorner.com).

"Potential home buyers will walk through your home in three to four minutes," says Selinger-Eaton. "Let's make those moments memorable and profitable!"

Selinger-Eaton's definition of staging is going into the home and taking things out that make the home look smaller, drab, or dated. Decorating is adding things to enhance the look of the home.

According to Selinger-Eaton, it's completely unnecessary to spend thousands of dollars for a stager to pull out all your furniture and bring in new. In fact, she believes that such tactics are giving staging a bad name.

"Everything you need to stage your home to sell quickly is there," says Selinger-Eaton. "For example, one broker wanted me to replace an ugly pink couch in a seller's home. Instead of charging the client $3,500 for a new couch, I got six chocolate brown pillows from Target, and repainted the peach walls. She couldn't believe it was the same couch."

That's the way to look at staging; you should spend money that is only going to make you money, make your house sell faster, and get multiple bids, if possible.

"My feeling is pick the right broker first, price the house right second," says Selinger-Eaton, "and third is stage it."

Staging is designed to decorate rooms to make them look larger and warmer, and thus increase the value of the home, by preparing your house as if your buyers are welcome guests. It can be as simple or as major as you can afford, but staging should include a decorating allowance as well as some tough love toward furniture or accessories that need to be shown the door.

These are among the questions to ask yourself when you are considering items to keep or replace or move around while staging your home:

- Is this item hurting the flow, size, or appearance of my home?

- Will it work better in another location or not at all?

- Can it be minimized or disguised with a throw blanket, pillows, or cloth?

- Will getting rid of this item make my house appear less cluttered?

- Does this item help tell a story that will help sell my home?

For example, any home might benefit from a new welcome mat, updated towels and mats in the baths, and candles strategically placed around the home. Set the dining room table for a formal candlelight dinner. Set the breakfast table with colorful pottery. Get rid of old bedding and replace with inexpensive but new-looking "beds in a bag," which you can find at department stores. Pillows work wonders. So does getting rid of discolored or dated looking lamps and replacing them.

Minor staging expenses might include:

- New bed treatment for master bedroom.
- Fresh flowers.
- New towels.
- Fresh paint in a trendy color—chocolate, silver sage, or one dramatic lacquer red wall.
- Replacing old lamps, or at least replacing lampshades.
- Powerwashing windows, doors.

Medium expenses in staging might include:

- Fresh paint throughout, inside and out.
- Replacing wallpaper with faux paints.
- New carpet (think darker—butterscotch instead of white).
- Fresh new bedding for all beds.

Major expenses in staging might include:

- Replacing old countertops with granite or Corian.
- Adding stainless appliances, glazed cupboards, gas cooktops.
- Renovating or adding hardwood floors.
- Changing old cabinet knobs to nickel or chrome.
- Replacing old brass bathroom mirror lighting.

- Replacing pedestal sinks with sink inset in footed furniture-style cabinet.

- Replacing outdated tile.

- Bringing in a grout specialist to replace or paint out dark, discolored grout.

Staging and Editing

Staging can include editing your furniture, accessories, and paint tones to complement the architecture and personality of your home. One way to accomplish this is to use staging to stimulate the imagination of the buyer through "scenes." For example, you can draw attention to a small study or den by posting a leather reading chair with a lamp table by the fireplace. This vignette would be staged by adding a pair of eyeglasses and the latest bestseller propped open with a handsome bookmark on the table. Now, the room is no longer small—it's cozy.

Here are eight ways to prepare your home's interior for marketing that you can do right now:

1. Along with getting rid of clutter on tables and other surfaces, get rid of stored clutter. Closets, bookshelves, cabinets, and nooks can all appear too small if they're overstuffed.

2. Pack away out-of-season clothes, accessories, sports equipment, and other things you won't be needing right away.

3. Consider renting a storage unit to store things you either won't be needing or don't want to use for showings.

4. As mentioned previously, consider staging your home. Your real estate agent can also offer suggestions to you to make the home more buyer-friendly.

5. Move pieces of furniture that clutter your home to the storage unit.

6. For major painting, don't skimp on the ceiling. Try painting trim a contrasting shade for higher impact. Keep white to a minimum. Color is in.

7. Polish wood cabinets, banisters, and windows.

8. Clean windows inside and out until they sparkle.

Preparing for Showings

As real estate expert and sales trainer David Knox (www.david knox.com), says, owners must know the importance of converting their home from *living* condition to *showing* condition.

"The critical thing to know is that buyers are selecting property on condition as well as price," says Knox, "and that's simply because most buyers want to close and move right in. If they have to visualize doing a lot of work before they move in, it turns them off."

That's not to say there isn't a place for the fixer-upper. But your market is going to be limited to do-it-yourselfers, first-time home buyers, and investors, all of whom are looking for bargains in exchange for doing the work themselves. But if your buyer is looking for a home to move into, you'll be better off if your home is "move-in ready."

Knox teaches real estate agents how to train sellers to prepare their homes for sale—using the five senses. Everyone wants a clean home. Your home must:

- Appear clean.
- Smell clean.
- Feel clean.

Decorate and update for general appeal. You don't want buyers coming into your home asking their agents what it will cost to tear out or repaint what you've done.

"People buy on emotion and decide on logic," says Knox. "You only have a second to make a first impression." Make sure the first impression isn't the smell of dog, ashtrays, or air freshener. Make sure cabinet doors aren't sticky to the touch, and that countertops are clean when buyers run their hands across to feel the texture.

"Certain things about the property you can't do anything about, and that is reflected in the price, such as noisy streets," says Knox, "but even busy streets all have someone living on them."

Accent the positive. You may be in a flight path, but you may also have one of the largest yards in the city. Your street may be busy, but it may also lead to some of the best shopping and entertainment around.

In other words, every house can sell.

Fresh-Baked Cookies and Other Ways to Relax the Subconscious

Many staging ideas are used for showings, such as leaving fresh-baked cookies on the kitchen counter, or lighting fragranced candles in bedrooms and baths, and there are many other ideas that can be productive, too. The idea is to make the buyer feel, remember something good from their childhood, and get the urge to make your home their home.

- Turn on all lights (high-wattage bulbs where possible) even for daytime showings.
- Open drapes, shutters, and blinds to let in light.
- Put on some relaxing music.
- Get rid of stale odors by opening windows, putting boxes of baking soda in the refrigerator, and put real charcoal in areas that absorb smells such as garages and kitchens. Be careful of perfumes, potpourri, wall-plug scents, or other masking products that could offend people with allergies.
- Clean fireplaces thoroughly and place candles on the grate.
- Keep countertops and table tops as clutter free as possible, including putting away small appliances, knickknacks, and collectibles.

- Put away family photos and other personal memorabilia.

- Remove prescription drugs before all showings.

- Put valuables such as fine jewelry, important papers, and other small items in a safe-deposit box.

- For unscheduled showings, do a five-minute pickup around the house before you leave every morning. Make sure all family members make their beds and have their rooms tidy. Put dirty clothes into the hamper. Don't let dishes accumulate in the sink.

Keep in mind that staging is a great way to enhance the market appeal of your home, but stay realistic. You're not going to turn a cottage into a mansion by moving a love seat into a small living room and removing the overstuffed sofa. You are, however, showing the buyer how to make the most out of the home's size, features, and style. And who knows? The buyer may like what you've done so much, they may ask you to throw in the loveseat when they make their offer!

CHAPTER 5

Market Realities

As you recall from Chapter 1, three things sell a house—location, condition, and price. Real estate markets have a way of taking advantage of sellers' weaknesses and rewarding their strengths. If you chose a good location, maintained the structure and grounds, and updated your home to compete with the features and look of newer homes, your property should compete well in any market.

To capitalize on your situation, it's important for you to understand buyers, how significant competition is from new and neighboring homes, and how housing markets really work.

Understanding Buyers and Their Motivations to Buy a Home

Consumers' relatively easy access to mortgages with little or no down payment; federal, state, and local tax incentives to own homes; and housing's consistent performance as an inflation-beater have all contributed to today's home buyers viewing home ownership as an important asset in their wealth-building portfolios.

Despite the ups and downs of local markets, there has never been a year since 1968, when NAR first starting keeping track, that housing nationwide has dipped below the rate of inflation, and it usually handily beats inflation by at least 1 to 2 percent.

Just as you are hoping to make a profit on your home, buyers are hoping they will choose a home that will appreciate in value. But there are other reasons buyers choose homes. Many buyers want the satisfaction and pride of owning their own homes. Some want more space while others want to scale down. Some buyers have been transferred or taken new jobs that put them in new environments. Many also want to live near family and friends. Second home buyers want vacation homes or investment properties.

What's important to know is if buyers can qualify to buy your home. As most will choose to use a mortgage loan, you should be able to keep unqualified buyers from tying up your property by insisting that they are qualified by a lender to buy your home. Before any offers are negotiated, insist on knowing whether a buyer has been preapproved for a mortgage loan. Buyers who have not been preapproved for financing pose a great risk of not being able to close on a property.

What Buyers Want in Homes

Buyers are willing to pay a premium for getting what they want. Overwhelmingly, NAR's most recent study of home buyers found that they ranked neighborhood quality (68 percent) as the most important factor in choosing a home.

Other considerations were:

- Proximity to job/school—43 percent.
- Close to friends/family—36 percent.
- School district—23 percent.
- Shopping—19 percent.
- Parks/recreation—15 percent.
- Planned community amenities—11 percent.
- Entertainment venues—9 percent.
- Public transportation—6 percent.
- Proximity to airport—6 percent.
- Health facilities—6 percent.

This is important for you to know because as long as they have choices, buyers are unlikely to compromise on the neighborhood, size, or features that they want most. The closer your home meets today's buyer checklist, the more likely it is that you will sell your home quickly, easily, and for the most money for your current market conditions.

The Allure of Newer Homes

While most homes purchased in 2005 were previously owned homes, one in five homes purchased were new construction. Buyers gravitated overwhelmingly toward newer homes.

New homes, whether custom-built or ready-to-move-into, are usually larger than previously owned homes and have features many home buyers want such as higher ceilings, central air-conditioning systems, and oversized garages.

Size Matters

Like many other aspects of American life, homes have upsized over the decades and are nearly double in square footage from what they were in 1950. One-third of home buyers bought between 1,501 and 2,000 square feet, while 11 percent of home buyers purchased homes more than 3,000 square feet.

First-time home buyers tended to buy smaller homes, most probably as a concession to price. Size is so important that one-third of home buyers reported that they did not compromise on factors such as neighborhood quality or size when making their home purchase. Newer homes are more likely to have the space and features buyers want.

Room Preferences

Not only is size important to home buyers, but so is the interior design of the home they buy. Buyers of existing homes were more likely to desire living rooms, basements, and sun rooms, while buyers of new homes valued home offices, media rooms, and homes with four or more bedrooms.

Nearly four in five buyers wanted a garage. More than 70 percent wanted two or more full bathrooms and a laundry room. More than 60 percent wanted a family room and formal dining room. One-third wanted a den/study, attic (storage), four or more bedrooms, basement, and utility room.

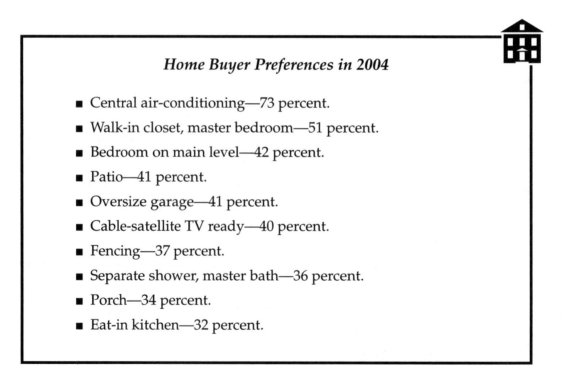

Home Buyer Preferences in 2004

- Central air-conditioning—73 percent.
- Walk-in closet, master bedroom—51 percent.
- Bedroom on main level—42 percent.
- Patio—41 percent.
- Oversize garage—41 percent.
- Cable-satellite TV ready—40 percent.
- Fencing—37 percent.
- Separate shower, master bath—36 percent.
- Porch—34 percent.
- Eat-in kitchen—32 percent.

What You Should Expect as a Seller

As you sell a previously owned home, expect home buyers to want to make changes to the home to meet their needs. Kitchens and baths are the two areas that home buyers most frequently plan to remodel, but home buyers seldom tackle these jobs soon after moving in. Only 15 percent of home buyers remodel within the first two years of owning their home, most likely because they are using all their resources to get into the best home they can possibly afford. This is why having an updated home is important; the less money the buyer has to budget for the unknowns of remodeling, the more he will be able to put toward the home. Needless to say, the more features your home offers compared to buyers' stated preferences, the better it will compete with other homes, even new homes, on the market.

Don't despair if you are in an older neighborhood; many existing homes are much more desirable to buyers for many reasons—the established surroundings; mature trees; size of the lot; proximity to jobs, shopping, and schools; the charm or rarity of period appointments such as crown moldings, hardwood floors, and so much more. In fact, many real estate professionals report that existing homes are in such demand that established neighborhoods sell at a premium. Some home buyers are rebelling against long commutes to faraway suburbs and are returning to older neighborhoods with an eye to contributing to revitalization and quality of life.

Understanding How Housing Markets Work

Housing markets are in a constant state of flux. They're impacted by a wide range of factors including economic and housing development, business growth, opportunity, availability, and mortgage interest rates and products. Buyers and sellers can interpret what's happening in a local market and drive it into a heated boom or a dusty bust.

Housing has been booming since the late 1990s, primarily due to the extremely homeowner-friendly Tax Relief Act of 1997. This Act allows homeowners to sell their homesteads and keep their capital gains up to $250,000 for singles, and $500,000 for couples, after living in their homes only two out of the previous five years of ownership.

This means a family could buy a home, live in it only two years, and after five years of ownership, keep all the gains from selling the home. Not only did homeownership soar for families, but also for singles who found it more feasible to own their own homes.

Every year since 2001 has ended in housing reaching new records, causing some economists to wonder if the entire nation is in a housing bubble.

According to David Lereah, chief economist for NAR, the housing boom has taken place because of six key factors, which he outlines in his book *Are You Missing the Housing Boom?* (Doubleday, 2005):

1. Mortgage interest rates dropped to generational lows.
2. Housing finance innovations lowered home ownership costs.
3. Home listings were centralized on the Internet.
4. Minority home ownership became a government priority.
5. Demographic influences (e.g., the maturing of the baby boom generation) strengthened housing demand.
6. Real estate became a safe haven for household wealth.

Lereah feels that, because most of these influences have not diminished, the nation's housing boom will continue through the end of the decade, even if it might show some signs of resting or plateauing at times or in certain locales.

However, while real estate can be affected by national events, it is impacted by your local market much more. What matters to you is what's happening in your particular market. It may be experiencing a boom, a plateau, or a decline. No matter what the market is like, there's a strategy for you that will help you sell your home for the highest price and best terms possible.

Buyer's and Seller's Markets

According to Lereah, real estate property appreciates for two reasons:

1. Market conditions create upward pressure on prices (e.g., demand exceeds supply).

2. Home improvements or renovations to a property, or an improvement to a neighborhood, add to a property's selling price.

As a seller, you must pay attention to the local market: Is your town creating jobs, bringing the migration of new households to your area? Or is your area closing plants and laying off workers?

As people create demand in the market, housing becomes more scarce, and prices go up. That's called a seller's market. These are characterized by strong buyer demand, low inventory, inventory that sells very quickly, multiple bids on properties, rising prices, and few if any concessions by sellers.

A buyer's market favors the buyer because there's not as much demand for housing. A buyer's market is characterized by lots of inventory, seller concessions and incentives, and prices that drift slowly lower.

If you look at housing markets as a scale, such as you will find on REALTOR.com's Market Conditions Reports, you will see that a buyer's market is at one end while a seller's market is at the other end. Let's say in a buyer's market, it takes one year to sell a home, while in a seller's market, it takes one day to sell a home.

If you use six months as the median, then markets that take longer than six months to sell a home are buyer's markets, and those that take less than six months to sell a home are seller's markets.

This is important for you to know because you need to know what is normal for your market. Knowing what to expect can help you and your agent price and market your home properly, and for the best results.

Market Values

Current market values can quickly change. All it takes is the announcement by a major employer in the area that the company is adding or eliminating jobs, and real estate will take an immediate turn for the better or worse. It all depends on how secure buyers feel about their finances. And lenders, too.

Contrary to popular belief, banks offer mortgage loans to buyers not because of the value of the property, but because of the borrower's ability to repay the loan with interest. So a mortgage loan is against income. Banks have no wish to operate or take back properties that collateralized the loans.

When people feel secure in their jobs and the economy, they spend money. When they feel uncertain or threatened that they will lose their jobs, they slow down their spending. This is true in housing, too.

Knowing what kind of market you're in is crucial to helping you set the asking price of your home.

Setting the Right Price

Pricing your home to sell is so important that the information in Chapter 3 bears repeating and further example.

When you were first given a CMA, your real estate agent analyzed your home compared to similar homes that had sold recently and properties currently on the market that would compete for the same buyers. The report also noted DOM or days on market.

The longer a home lingers on the market, the less likely it is to fetch the original asking price. You want to sell quickly to get the highest, best price.

Your job as the seller is to make the house as attractive as possible to as many buyers as you can. As you've already learned, location, condition, and price are the way to a buyer's heart.

The most important of these is price. It must reflect the current market conditions. Your home is worth only what a willing buyer will pay for it. When you expose your home to the marketplace, you and your agent will use as many resources as possible to find the right buyer. If you find you aren't getting offers, price is most often the problem.

Three out of four buyers use a real estate agent of their own, and it's likely that if they are interested in your home, they will be considering a CMA that has been prepared for them by their buyer's agent. These buyers will use the CMA to consider the properties on the market. If your home offers the most value, it will sell quickly. If there are other homes that offer more value for less money than your home, it will not sell, or you will find yourself fielding far lower offers than you expected.

To keep your expectations reasonable, consider the following:

- Appraisals, tax assessments, and CMAs don't determine market value—buyers do.
- Almost all home buyers look at buying a home as an investment.
- Homes needing improvement will not fetch the price of similar, nicely maintained homes.

What you need to "net" from the home to meet personal goals has nothing to do with what a buyer may offer for your home. Home buyers can't be expected to pay for your retirement, your child's college, or family vacations. Buyers will pay what they feel your home is worth in the current market.

Home buyers expect the seller to make some profit, but buyers are thinking of themselves. If they pay too much for your home, they won't be able to resell for as much profit.

If you've used your home like an ATM, through the use of equity loans, without spending money for home improvement, don't necessarily expect to recoup the extra amount you owe by increasing the price of your home. If you haven't done the maintenance to keep your home up-to-date, you most likely will not receive top dollar for it.

Cosmetic touch-ups are expected by buyers. Paint can be helpful, for example, but it should be neutral. Buyers want to picture the home the way they want it, not with a color the seller thinks is attractive. Any improvements you make should be carefully considered, as the buyer will calculate the cost of redoing what you've done if they don't like your taste.

Poorly maintained homes take more of a market beating in buyer's markets because nicer homes are available at bargain prices. On the other hand, a rising market will lift all houses.

A lot of headaches can be saved by having the home professionally inspected so that you are not blindsided by unexpected problems and repairs found by the buyer and her inspector. A preemptive inspection allows you to make the repairs and assists you with providing a more accurate disclosure. A seller's disclosure statement will alert the buyer to issues that you know of and have addressed or do not know of, for which the buyer needs to be on the lookout to investigate themselves and through their buyer's inspection.

How to Get the Most Money for Your Home

To achieve the best asking price:

■ *Don't use your home as an ATM.* If you take money out of your home in the form of a loan, make sure you make improvements to the home that keep it current by today's market standards.

■ *Keep your home in top condition.* All homes show signs of wear, but keeping your home in good repair means you can sell at a moment's notice without a make-ready period, and fetch top dollar for your home.

■ *Don't be offended by low offers.* The better condition your home is in, the more likely you will be offered close to your asking price. Low offers are characteristic of buyer's markets, where there is lots of competition by other similar homes, or such offers are a reflection of the condition of your home compared to similar but better maintained homes.

■ *Don't let your emotions or greed affect the price of your home.* Beauty is in the eye of the beholder, and that is why almost all sellers are tempted to overprice their homes. A high price is prestigious, but it may eliminate the very buyer you need.

■ *Don't overvalue personal improvements.* Everybody customizes a home when they move in. You like wallpaper, another likes faux paints. You like open spaces, someone else may favor nooks and crannies. People have different tastes and priorities.

(Continued)

How to Get the Most Money for Your Home (Continued)

That swimming pool you put in for $30,000 is terrific, but the next buyer may view it as a financial drain or major insurance liability especially if it is more than 10 years old. You see, improvements age, and when they age, they can become repair and maintenance headaches.

It's best to look upon improvements as something you did to please yourself, but don't expect all updates to add value to the home.

- *Don't mistake activity for offers.* When people are interested, they make offers. If they aren't making offers, something is holding them back. Many agents routinely ask for feedback whenever your home is shown, but a lot of agents don't follow through with this courtesy. But feedback is crucial to understanding why you aren't getting offers on the home. The lack of response is usually due to two things: The home is in poor condition and/or it is overpriced.

- *Prepare your home for success.* Preparing the home for sale can include everything from spring cleaning, to repainting, to clearing out clutter, to making repairs, and so on. It's hard work!

Many people leave their exteriors and interiors as is, but if you haven't updated in years and the home looks outdated, it will not compare as well as others who have taken the time and gone to the expense to freshen the home. Also keep in mind that you are competing not only with other homes in the neighborhood but with new homes as well.

Today's buyer wants what the new homes have. If they can't get it, they will settle for a mature home with a fresh look and everything in working order. The home must "feel new."

Avoid Obstacles to Selling

Make your home available for showings as much as possible. Buyers may have limited times to view your home—after work or on the weekends, when you'd prefer to relax. One of the reasons you have an agent is to show your home for you. You don't have to be present.

In fact, agents usually prefer for you not to be there for two main reasons: Buyers like to feel at home and won't be comfortable opening closet doors and kitchen cabinets with you in sight. Staying longer in a home and thoroughly checking it out are signs a buyer likes your home.

In addition, you don't want to be in a position of inadvertently giving information that could hurt your negotiating position. A likely question that you might get from a buyer is, "Why are you selling?" Your answer could mean a lot. What if you were to tell the buyer you're being transferred or that you're purchasing another home? You might convey a sense of urgency that could give the buyer the negotiating advantage that could delay reaching an agreement.

Another way to delay your home's sale is to try to restrict the times that your agent can show your home, so you can continue life as usual. Many showings might occur at dinnertime, for example. You must think in terms of when buyers are available to view homes, and for many, that will be after work, on Saturdays and Sundays—the same times you would like to relax in privacy. Unfortunately, you can't expect your agent to reschedule showings to a more convenient time, because there may not be such a time.

Avoid layering contingencies onto the contract. With a choice between your home and another similar home, a buyer will look more closely at terms. If you want to sell but don't want the buyer to take possession until your new home is built, that's a contingency that asks a lot of the buyer. Why not move your things into storage and make the sale cleaner and simpler for everyone? The buyer may have contingencies, too, such as waiting to move until the school year is over. If you can accommodate the buyer, that's a bargaining chip.

What If Your Home Isn't Selling?

It is easy to get frustrated if your home does not sell right away. Many sellers suspect that it might be due to lack of effort on their agent's part and want to take action immediately. Before you make any major changes with the marketing of your home, which will cause even further delays, take some time to review the situation clearly.

If you followed previous advice and asked your agent for a complete marketing plan, you can review the plan to see if all the actions your agent promised occurred on schedule. If your agent isn't in touch, simply call, leave a message, or write an e-mail.

During busy seasons, such as spring and summer while home buyers are trying to get moved before school starts, your agent may be operating at peak load. That's no excuse for the agent failing to be in touch. Don't be afraid to remind your agent that the listing agreement requires him to provide regular updates on the marketing of your home, as well as how your local market is doing overall.

Depending on your market, things could have changed for the better or the worse. Chances are, if you aren't hearing anything from your agent, your home is not being shown. This could be potentially disastrous; if you aren't getting showings, you won't get any offers, and your home could even end up selling for less than it would have if you had set the listing price lower. See David Knox's stairstep chart.

Think back. Did you choose the listing price? Most likely you did from a range recommended by your agent, or you might have insisted on listing it at a higher price.

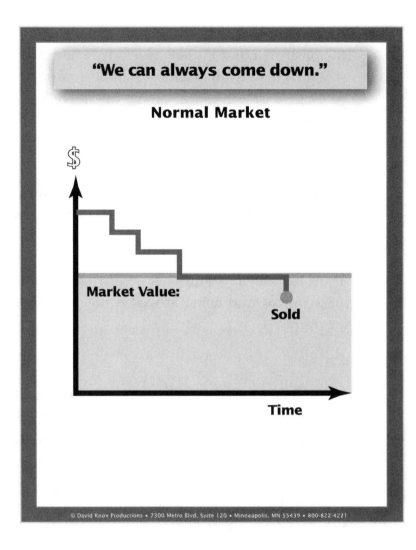

If so, here's what may have gone wrong, according to David Knox. Often in listing negotiations, sellers will have three strategies they want to try, and it takes a strong agent to disagree.

1. *"Couldn't we try listing it at the higher price for a couple of weeks?"* Says Knox, "Almost all your showings occur within the first and second week, because most people want to see the *new* listings. If you're overpriced during the period when you have the most activity, that means you are lowering your price after all the people have gone."

2. *"Well, we can always come down."* Knox says, "When buyers look at houses, the first thing they ask is, 'How long has this home been on the market?' You'll sell it for less the longer it remains on the market because the buyer will think there's something wrong with it, or that they don't have any competition to buy it. Either way, they'll make lower offers."

3. *"People can always make an offer."* Knox's response? "They'll make an offer only if they see your house. If your home is worth $400,000 and you price it at $450,000, the right buyers won't see it and the higher priced buyers don't want it. The people looking at $450,000 homes will see that your home doesn't compare."

The bottom line? Even the best agent in the world can't sell your home for more than it's worth, although your agent may try.

If you believe that your agent isn't living up to your agreement, and isn't responding to requests for information, call the agent's broker and explain your concerns. Your listing contract is with the broker so it is perfectly appropriate to ask for attention and remedies from the broker, rather than (or in addition to) your agent.

Five Ways to Speed Up Your Sale

1. Price it right. Set a price at the lower end of your property's realistic price range.

2. Get your house market-ready for at least two weeks before you begin showing it.

3. Be flexible about showings. It's often disruptive to have a house ready to show on the spur of the moment, but the more often someone can see your home, the sooner you'll find a seller.

4. Be ready for the offers. Decide in advance what price and terms you'll find acceptable.

5. Don't refuse to drop the price. If your home has been on the market for more than 30 days without an offer, be prepared to lower your asking price.

(Copyright 2006. Reprinted with permission from REALTOR® Magazine Online.)

CHAPTER 6

Security and Other Issues with Marketing Your Home

One of the most important reasons you hire a real estate agent is to protect your interests while marketing your home. That includes demonstrating care, common sense, and caution with regard to letting strangers into your home.

You can include in your listing contract that your agent and any cooperating agents who wish to show your home open it only to qualified prospects.

A qualified buyer is someone who has shared their financial history with a lender and is ready to buy a home now. The lender evaluates the information and suggests an appropriate price range for which the buyer can be assured of getting a loan.

A buyer who has been qualified by a lender is a ready buyer. You want to welcome ready buyers to your home, but discourage anyone else who isn't actively interested in helping you sell your home from bothering you or your agent.

Ways Buyers Search for Homes

According to the *2005 NAR Profile of Home Buyers and Sellers*, most buyers spend about eight weeks actively searching for a home, and they typically view about nine homes before making a selection.

As mentioned in Chapter 2, the Internet plays a strong role in buyers' home searches.

- Overall, 57 percent of all home buyers use the Internet to search for a home.
- Of first-time home buyers, 82 percent use the Internet to search for a home.
- From 1997 to 2005, the percentage of home buyers who first found the home they purchased on the Internet has increased from 2 percent to 24 percent.

About 90 percent of buyers use their own real estate agent. Other methods they use to find information on homes include:

Internet—77 percent.

Yard signs—71 percent.

Open houses—51 percent.

Newspaper advertisements—50 percent.

Home books or magazines—38 percent.

Home builders—36 percent.

Television—25 percent.

Billboards—19 percent.

Relocation companies—15 percent.

As you can see, your greatest chance of finding a buyer is through agents, advertising, and open houses.

Now, compare how buyers found the home they decided to purchase:

Real estate agent—36 percent.

Internet—24 percent.

Yard sign—15 percent.

Friends, neighbors, relatives—7 percent.

Home builder or agent—7 percent.

Newspaper ad—5 percent.

Knew the seller—3 percent.

Home book or magazine—1 percent.

The Value of Agents

Because agents are neighborhood experts, many will know your neighborhood and perhaps have personal knowledge of your home. Perhaps they remember when it was listed when you bought it.

It's your agent's job to offer to list your home in the MLS, which is important. According to NAR, 90 percent of home buyers used a real estate agent during their home search, so it's crucial that other agents know the latest information about your home including any changes to your listing.

Your agent may put your home on "tour," where agents come to preview homes without their customers. Agent tours can be sociable events with coffee and snacks for your guests.

Increasingly, agents are also turning to the Internet to preview homes for their customers. As you can see from the preceding information, the Internet is the key way to view, preview, eliminate, or choose properties to consider for agents and their buyers.

The Internet Listing

Successful agents use many marketing channels to present your home to the marketplace, including the Internet. Among the tools your agent may use are multiple photos, floor plans, virtual tours, and video commercials that can be shown on TV and online.

Your home should be in move-in-ready condition when you begin marketing, and that means it should be camera-ready because marketing begins with the entry of the listing into the MLS and in public advertising on sites like REALTOR.com.

Your agent will either take photos or hire a professional photographer/videographer. Generally speaking, most agents won't enter the home into the MLS without accompanying photos (and photos are mandatory for some MLSs), so the sooner your home is ready for its close-up, the faster you can start marketing.

Virtual tours are effectively being used to market homes because the technology allows the buyer to peruse rooms and features at their own pace. Using a fish-eye lens or other photo stitching technologies, virtual tours can literally provide a 360 degree look at all angles of a room, home, or neighborhood. Many have zoom features so you can get a close-up of that fireplace or crown molding. Virtual tours are wonderful to use for selection and elimination of homes.

Still photos significantly impact online marketing as well. As mentioned earlier, most buyers start their search for homes on the Internet. Many buyers won't look at online advertisements without photos as they assume there must be something wrong with the house. While this is generally not true, the old adage about first impressions being the ones that matter can be created through an online advertisement.

One advantage to advertising your home on the Internet is that the buyer can learn a lot about your home without disturbing you. Pictures are worth a thousand words, but the Internet can carry so much more information than ordinary print ads. You can add room dimensions and more details about your property. Internet innovations include information or links that can be extremely helpful to buyers such as satellite views of the neighborhood and property, school reports, and amenities such as parks, services, and shopping.

The Internet is a wonderful tool because:

- Agents can send their customers e-mail alerts that include information about your home.
- Agents can prepare fliers for your home that include directions to which web sites have information on your home.
- Buyers can peruse the Internet again and again and use comparison features to put your home in competition with another.
- Research shows that buyers who use the Internet overwhelmingly choose homes they first saw there.

The number one visited web site for homes on the Internet is REALTOR.com, NAR's official consumer web site. Due to the unique relationship that NAR has with the nation's nearly 900 multiple listing services, REALTOR.com offers more listings for consumers to view online than any other single source.

Unlike some web sites, which require consumers to register before giving them access to listings or to real estate agents so that the consumers can ask questions about the listings, REALTOR.com publishes the phone number and web site of every listing broker whose listings are online. Agents can enhance their listings with multiple photos, virtual tours, and other features to attract buyers to your home. When a consumer has a question, they can e-mail the agent directly from the advertisement—your online listing.

Your agent or the agent's MLS may also have relationships with other service providers to advertise your listing online. Again, it should be outlined in your marketing plan.

Agent and Buyer Etiquette, Netiquette, or Lack Thereof

No professional agent should come to your door or call you directly (unless your listing states to call you directly for showing appointments), when you are represented by a listing agent. If a buyer's agent has questions or wishes to show your home, they should contact your agent, not you.

It does happen, however, that an unscrupulous agent may try to contact you and tell you that your agent has underpriced the home or is making some other mistake with your listing. If you withdraw the listing and list your home with them, you'll get more money for your home, they promise. Or they may say they have a buyer for the home, but they don't want to share their commission with the listing agent. Don't believe them. These are not reputable people, and not likely to be members of your agent's association and MLS. Report activities like this to your agent.

What to Do about Unrepresented Buyers. Sometimes first-time home buyers are just starting the home buying process and may not understand that you are represented by an agent. They may knock on your door, cheerfully waving a feature sheet of your home that they downloaded from your agent's Internet ad, not realizing that they should have contacted your agent (or found their own agent) for an appointment to see your home.

Simply explain that only your agent schedules showings. Give them your agent's card and a flier about your home if they don't already have one. Don't answer questions about the home, so you won't inadvertently give away a bargaining chip. Be friendly but firm, and tell them you hope they'll schedule an appointment soon.

A Word about Solicitations. If you see that as soon as your listing is entered into the MLS, your mailbox starts filling up with moving company solicitations and other junk mail, tell your agent.

It's an unfortunate price for access to the MLS that some would sell your information for money, but that's how it is in the Wild Wild West that is the Internet. Information can be "scraped" including your listing from the MLS.

MLS organizations have strict rules about protecting sellers and are doing their best to try to keep such things from happening.

The best defense is to report this information and give any unsolicited material to your agent so the incident can be investigated through the proper channels.

Your agent will do her best to protect you during showings by keeping records of people who have inquired about your home or have seen your home through showings, public open houses, and agent open houses. That way you know who is interested in your home or has been in your home.

For your own personal protection as well as that of your belongings, don't let anyone in your home without prior knowledge that they have an appointment made through your agent.

Open Houses

A time-honored tradition, the open house is a two- to four-hour showing of your home that is open to the public. It's a great way for buyers to see neighborhood homes while they are still in the idea-gathering stage, but open houses aren't necessarily the most direct way to help you find a buyer for your home.

However, open houses can be invaluable in starting or continuing buzz about your home. This is one area where a print ad is helpful—to advertise that your home will be open. You may get a lot of lookie-loos—people who don't intend to buy, but who just want to see your decorating ideas or how their home compares to yours.

It's hard to keep neighbors away. You want the word spread about your home from people who are already enthusiastic about living there, but some neighbors may come just to snoop. There's always that chance, however, that they may know someone who is looking to buy in the neighborhood. Your agent may go to your neighbors as part of the marketing plan and tell them about your home and invite them to come to an open house.

Seven Steps to Preparing for an Open House

1. Hire a cleaning service. A spotlessly clean home is essential; dirt will turn off a prospect faster than anything.

2. Mow your lawn, and be sure toys and yard equipment are put away.

3. Serve cookies, coffee, and soft drinks. It creates a welcoming touch. But be sure the kitchen has been cleaned up; use disposable cups so the sink doesn't fill up.

4. Lock up your valuables, jewelry, and money. Although the real estate salesperson will be on site during the open house, it's impossible to watch everyone all the time.

5. Turn on all the lights. Even in the daytime, incandescent lights add sparkle.

7. Send your pets to a neighbor or take them outside. If that's not possible, crate them or confine them to one room (a basement or bath), and let the salesperson know where to find them.

8. It's awkward for prospective buyers to look in your closets and express their opinions of your home with you there.

(Copyright 2006. Reprinted with permission from REALTOR® Magazine Online.)

Another note about showings and open houses. Make sure you put away your prescription drugs. Some sellers have returned after an open house to find their medication has been stolen. Remove any firearms or weapons you may have in the house as well. This also provides additional protection for your agent in case he or she is alone in the house with someone who decides to try something.

Ten Ways to Make Your Home Irresistible at an Open House

1. Put fresh or silk flowers in principal rooms for a touch of color.

2. Add a new shower curtain, fresh towels, and new guest soaps to every bath.

3. Set out potpourri or fresh-baked goods for a homey smell.

4. Set the table with pretty dishes and candles.

5. Buy a fresh doormat with a clever saying.

6. Take one or two major pieces of furniture out of every room to create a sense of spaciousness.

7. Put away kitchen appliances and personal bathroom items to give the illusion of more counter space.

8. Lay a fire in the fireplace. Or put a basket of flowers there if it's not in use.

9. Depersonalize the rooms by putting away family photos, mementos, and distinctive artwork.

10. Turn on the sprinklers earlier in the day for 30 minutes to make the lawn sparkle.

(Copyright 2006. Reprinted with permission from REALTOR® Magazine Online.)

HOA Marketing Restrictions

Sometimes in the interest of exclusivity, a homeowners association (HOA) will have rules that prevent your home from appearing as if it's on the market.

These rules state that no signs in the windows or yard are allowed, and if you live in a gated community, you may find that there are certain procedures that agents and buyers must go through in order to enter the neighborhood.

You also may find it particularly challenging to sell a home if your building is owned by a management company that is also trying to sell units. On-site salespeople may forget to pass along your agent's card to prospective buyers. That's one of the dangers of condo conversions; you are always competing against the house.

The best way to deal with the HOA rules is simply to learn about them up front. Give a copy of your HOA's rules and the HOA's management contacts to your agent, and she will find out whom to call, how to schedule showings, and what's allowed/not allowed in marketing your home.

Because you won't have the advantage of yard signs, which is helpful to drive-by buyers, that means your agent will have to step up other marketing, especially Internet marketing. This should include directions on how to see the home.

Viral marketing—telling everyone you know that your home is for sale—is also helpful. You may be pleasantly surprised that friends have secretly coveted your neighborhood or your home and might be ready to make a move.

Expect marketing to take a little longer for homes that are under some sort of marketing restriction from homes that aren't, but it doesn't have to necessarily be so. It's all about price and location.

Fair Housing Laws

Because of the unique size, layout, décor, features, or neighborhood location of your home, you may personally feel that it is ideally suited for a particular kind of buyer, but beware.

Fair housing laws, found at www.hud.gov, strictly prohibit restricting consumers from the opportunity to buy or rent a home based on race, color, religion, sex, handicap, familial status, or national origin.

Fair housing laws protect classes of people from having housing opportunities denied them based on the color of their skin, a handicap, familial status, or other personal characteristic that has nothing to do with their economic ability to buy, sell, rent, or lease a home.

Again, this is another area where having an agent can make all the difference in the world. Agents are familiar with fair housing regulations and will make sure that your marketing complies.

You should know that as a home seller, you have a responsibility and a requirement under the law not to discriminate in the sale or financing of property on the basis of race, color, religion, sex, handicap, familial status, or national origin. You may not instruct your broker to convey for you any limitations on the sale because the broker is also bound by law not to discriminate.

Under the law, a seller cannot:

- Establish discriminatory terms or conditions in the purchase or rental of housing.
- Advertise a preference for certain buyers because of their race, color, religion, sex, handicap, familial status, or national origin.
- Misrepresent that housing is unavailable to persons who are members of these protected classes.

This is crucial for you to know, because you might be in a fee-for-service arrangement with a broker whereby you pay for and write some of the advertising for your home yourself.

If you are involved in creating the marketing for your listing, stay away from words and phrases that are indicative of race, color, religion, sex, handicap, familial status, or national origin. In addition, catchphrases like *exclusive, private,* or *traditional* also can be considered discriminatory.

But adding a disclaimer shouldn't be viewed as a bulletproof shield. The question to ask yourself when composing any ad or marketing material about your home, as suggested by Arizona real estate attorney Robert Bass, is, "Could what I'm doing be misconstrued as discriminatory?"

Keep in mind that buyer demographics are changing all the time. The ideal buyer for your home may surprise you. To stay on the safe side, keep any written descriptions focused on the property and its features.

CHAPTER 7

On the Market

Now it's showtime. Time to show your home, that is. You've priced your home and your broker has listed it in the MLS. Your agent is marketing to other brokers and to home buyers, and you've decluttered, painted, planted fresh flowers, and perhaps done some staging.

You're ready to welcome home buyers into your home. How will they react? That's a good question, and it depends on your individual market, how you've prepared your home for market, and what kind of buyers your home attracts.

Any buyer who is serious will look beyond the superficial. They want to know what's working, what needs replacing, and what needs to be fixed. That raises an interesting question: Should you get your home inspected?

Seller Home Inspections

Home inspectors are hired by buyers to ascertain the working condition of the structure, plumbing, electricity, and other systems before obligating themselves to buy.

The reason is that inspections can yield some surprises. If you've never gone under your house, you might be surprised to learn your foundation is sagging and that you need a few piers to shore up the floors. When the buyer finds the problem on their inspection, they can either ask to be released from the contract, ask you to fix the problem, or ask you to reduce the cost of the home so they can fix the problem themselves, according to what their lender will allow. (In certain parts of the country, it may be customary for the buyer to have an inspection prior to making an offer.)

Some problems are minor, but others can derail your transaction. As a seller, it would be nice to know what these problems are in advance. That's why it's a good idea to get a home inspection before putting your home up for sale.

A seller who is on the up-and-up will appear more trustworthy to buyers if they can see a copy of an inspection report, and what actions were taken to fix any problems that were unearthed. In this way, the seller can use the inspection report as a kind of handy punch-list of things to do to make the home more marketable.

Most buyers will still opt to have their own inspection, which may uncover the same blemishes or new ones. The point is that anything that isn't perfect on the report can serve to reopen negotiations.

The problem with getting a preinspection is that the findings should be disclosed to the buyer. It would be hard to say you didn't notice the sloping floors if it's right there on the report.

And that's where the dilemma comes in: Should you expose yourself to buyers who may want you to fix every little thing on the report? That's a question that should really be discussed with your agent, and the reason is no two inspectors will likely flag the same items on the same report, because they may have an opinion as to what should be included on an inspection report, obvious structural defects aside.

A lot will depend on your local market. If you live in a state that requires that you disclose what you know about the working features of the home, or you are in a strong seller's market with multiple offers and rising prices, your buyer may forgo having their own inspection based on the speed of the market and trusting that your disclosure is truthful.

If your state doesn't require a preinspection, or your market is moving into a buyer's market with more competition, it could be a benefit to provide a preinspection report to boost buyer confidence.

Your agent will make a recommendation to you but will never ask you to hide your knowledge of anything in the home that isn't working properly.

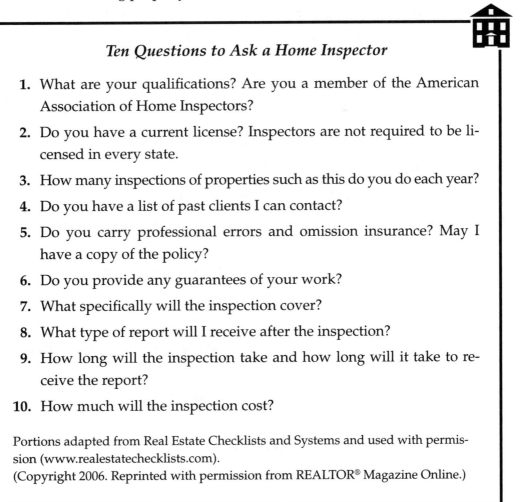

Ten Questions to Ask a Home Inspector

1. What are your qualifications? Are you a member of the American Association of Home Inspectors?

2. Do you have a current license? Inspectors are not required to be licensed in every state.

3. How many inspections of properties such as this do you do each year?

4. Do you have a list of past clients I can contact?

5. Do you carry professional errors and omission insurance? May I have a copy of the policy?

6. Do you provide any guarantees of your work?

7. What specifically will the inspection cover?

8. What type of report will I receive after the inspection?

9. How long will the inspection take and how long will it take to receive the report?

10. How much will the inspection cost?

Portions adapted from Real Estate Checklists and Systems and used with permission (www.realestatechecklists.com).
(Copyright 2006. Reprinted with permission from REALTOR® Magazine Online.)

If you are frightened of having a home inspection, that's a sure sign that you probably should have one. Like going to the doctor, you might be more afraid of the report than anything else, but look at it this way: It's far better to know what you're dealing with than to allow a problem to hit you between the eyes later on. If an inspection uncovers a problem, it is there and might only get worse. It has to be dealt with—either through repairs or negotiations.

What Your Home Inspection Should Cover

- *Siding:* Look for dents or buckling.

- *Foundations:* Look for cracks or water seepage.

- *Exterior brick:* Look for cracked bricks or mortar pulling away from bricks.

- *Insulation:* Look for condition, adequate rating for climate.

- *Doors and windows:* Look for loose or tight fits, condition of locks, condition of weatherstripping.

- *Roof:* Look for age, conditions of flashing, pooling water, buckled shingles, or loose gutters and downspouts.

- *Ceilings, walls, and moldings:* Look for loose pieces, drywall that is pulling away.

- *Porch/deck:* Look for loose railings or steps, rot.

What Your Home Inspection Should Cover (Continued)

- *Electrical:* Look for condition of fuse box/circuit breakers, number of outlets in each room.

- *Plumbing:* Look for poor water pressure, banging pipes, rust spots or corrosion that indicate leaks, insufficient insulation.

- *Water heater:* Look for age, size adequate for house, speed of recovery, energy rating.

- *Furnace/air-conditioning:* Look for age, energy rating. Furnaces are rated by annual fuel utilization efficiency; the higher the rating, the lower your fuel costs. However, keep other factors in mind such as payback period and other operating costs, such as electricity to operate motors.

- *Garage:* Look for exterior in good repair; condition of floor (cracks, stains, etc.); condition of door mechanism.

- *Basement:* Look for water leakage, musty smell.

- *Attic:* Look for adequate ventilation, water leaks from roof.

- *Septic tanks (if applicable):* Adequate absorption field capacity for the percolation rate in your area and the size of your family.

- *Driveways/sidewalks:* Look for cracks, heaving pavement, crumbling near edges, stains.

(Copyright 2006. Reprinted with permission from REALTOR® Magazine Online.)

Seller Disclosure Forms

In most states, sellers and their agents are obligated to disclose known material defects in a property to all potential purchasers. Sellers are in a better position to be aware of information about the condition of the property, and seller disclosure forms convey this knowledge to the purchaser. Use of seller disclosures can result in fewer surprises to purchasers after the closing, thereby reducing the likelihood of a lawsuit if something goes wrong with the home.

Purchasers who have used seller disclosure forms indicate that they closely review the information and find it to be useful. They also acknowledge that the forms allowed them to make faster purchases and more informed purchasing decisions. For instance, purchasers unfamiliar with the part of the country where they are purchasing property may find information in a disclosure form useful in making them aware of various idiosyncrasies that may affect property in that geographical area, such as the landslides common in some areas of California.

Purchasers provided with a property condition disclosure form generally are also likely to be more satisfied with their purchase because they are less likely to encounter surprises about the property's condition. Fewer surprises ultimately decrease the likelihood of litigation over a transaction. The use of a property condition disclosure form does not, however, diminish or eliminate the benefit of an independent home inspection. The disclosure form reveals what the seller actually knows about the condition of the property, while an inspection may reveal conditions or defects of which the seller may not be aware. Most forms, in fact, specifically suggest the value of an independent home inspection in addition to the disclosure form.

The seller benefits from use of the property condition disclosure form because it provides documentation of his disclosure to the purchaser of any problems with the property, thereby limiting potential future claims for misrepresentation. In addition, completing a seller disclosure form can help a seller identify home repairs or improvements that can be made to make the property sell more quickly and to generate the highest possible price.

As mentioned, most disclosure forms also recommend that the purchaser obtain an independent home inspection. When the purchaser follows that recommendation, the burden of determining the condition of major or more complex features or systems in the home, such as the electrical system, the roof, or the furnace, falls to an individual with requisite expertise rather than to the seller or agent. In such cases, the likelihood of claims against the seller is reduced and the seller's ability to defend against such claims is conversely enhanced.

However, your agent will take a look at your property before you list it to see if she notices anything out of the ordinary. If your agent notices something—like an obvious discoloration on the ceiling that might indicate a water leak, or major cracks in the wall—that is not marked on your seller disclosure form, your agent will ask about the inconsistency. Your agent will then modify the disclosure form as may be necessary.

Unless the law of a state imposes specific requirements, the completed form may be provided to prospective purchasers during the showing of the property, or disclosure may occur only after they express particular interest in the property. Disclosure forms may also be left in a visible location in the home for review during showings. In any case, a prospective purchaser must have the opportunity to read the form and seek any necessary additional information or clarification prior to making an offer. It is prudent to have your agent require the prospective purchaser to sign an acknowledgment indicating the purchaser's receipt of the disclosure form and information.

Who Are Your Buyers?

As you learned in earlier chapters, age and price range have a lot to do with what motivates buyers to buy a home, but there are other motivations as well.

Homes are simply rewarding investments for families. Not only do they provide a haven, they are memory-makers, too. Everyone remembers special things about their childhood home, or Grandma's house, or other places that provided a feeling of warmth and security. Some have dream homes in mind—places where they want to create their own memories. That's where your staging will pay dividends, by tapping into those emotions.

Luckily for most families, homes have also proven to be wise investments. Home ownership is strongly supported by the U.S. government, which provides lots of tax benefits, and other developments have encouraged more mobility, which improves the chances of finding buyers for your home.

As was mentioned in Chapter 5, the Tax Relief Act of 1997 encourages mobility by enabling homeowners to sell their homes after they've owned the property for five years with at least two years of occupation. The act allows owners to keep capital gains up to $250,000 for singles and $500,000 for married couples.

Unlike previous generations, when home buyers had to put down 20 percent or more in a down payment and were able to take advantage of tax-free gains only once in a lifetime, today's home buyers have experienced unprecedented appreciation in home values, particularly during periods and in areas when home sales and prices reached record-setting levels.

Of course, such times are ultimately unsustainable, and the market may react by taking a breather, but overall, housing has never retreated in price nationwide since NAR began keeping track in 1968. In fact, it has beaten inflation by at least one to two percentage points every year.

In some years, housing has outperformed other investments such as stocks and bonds while providing a number of added benefits—shelter, tax benefits, neighborhood, and so on.

That's why 94 percent of home buyers believe that a home purchase is a good investment. All of this has home buyers somewhat concerned about being able to jump in and out of their housing investment. This concern is supported by the number of years that homeowners tend to stay in their homes—about six years. Owners of townhomes, co-ops, or condominiums tend to move even more frequently.

You could say it's a generational thing, but with buying conditions so different, today's home buyers have grown up with different expectations than previous generations. This impacts their behavior and the way they negotiate with sellers.

Buyers have been conditioned to use credit, take risks, and get into a home as early as possible with the least amount of money feasible, a belief that has been widely encouraged by the easy availability of interest-only mortgages and other exotic loan products. According to the *2005 NAR Profile of Home Buyers and Sellers*, 92 percent of home buyers need to finance a portion of their purchase with a mortgage. The amount of the purchase that needed financing was a median of 87 percent nationwide. In addition, more than one out of four home buyers needed to finance the entire purchase.

Quick gains may be one of the reasons you're selling your home. Or you may need to trade up or down depending on the size of your family, so you will certainly be able to understand the motivations of a buyer who may be in your shoes. For example, approximately 60 percent of home buyers need to sell their home or have sold their home in order to buy your home.

Contingencies

These statistics should prepare you for the idea that some buyers may present a contract to you that is conditional on their home selling first, and that almost any buyer will have to make purchasing your home contingent upon securing financing.

Depending on your market, you may not have the patience to wait until a buyer sells his home before closing on yours. What you decide to accept is up to you, but buyers with good credit can get bridge loans to get them into your house until they sell theirs, so having a house to sell isn't necessarily a condition you have to accept. However, in a down market, where you are in a less-than-favorable negotiating position, conceding this condition to your buyer may make the difference to a successful transaction.

As far as financing goes, it's a little touchy to dig too deeply into the buyer's business, but you can certainly make it clear to your agent that you don't want your time wasted with buyers who aren't prepared to buy. You can ask that only prequalified home buyers view your home, and your agent will include that in the showing instructions.

Low-Ball Buyers

The fastest way to attract low-ball buyers is to market your home "as is." That means you have no intention of fixing anything that may be wrong with the home, which can tend to relay to buyers that there are multiple problems with the home from repairs to lack of updates. That can limit interested buyers except for those who are willing to tackle the unknowns of your home. On the other hand, there's an advantage to marketing directly to buyers whose eyes are wide open. They know that you are selling a fixer-upper, and negotiations should be short and sweet. However, keep in mind that selling as is doesn't absolve you from disclosing known defects.

You may find that home buyers don't think your home is worth what you and your agent thought it was—primarily because of the nature of unknowns. You carefully combed through comparables to come up with a sales price that you felt was fair to the market-place while still being attractive enough to bring the right buyer, but there are a lot of ifs with repairs and updates: Can you get the right contractor? What will materials costs? Can the home be improved the way the buyer envisions?

Whether you are marketing an as is or older unimproved or out-dated home, your agent can help you find the best buyers for your property. However, you can expect to run into the following types of buyers.

Speculators/Long-Term Investors.   While they can be assured of buying your home when all else fails (assuming you can't get your price), speculators and investors follow a profit formula that includes buying under the market or asking price, usually in the neighborhood of 15 to 20 percent lower. If a sales price doesn't fit this criteria, the investor moves on, because for them there is nothing emotional about the purchase.

This type of investor is usually experienced, buys and improves and flips numerous properties, and tends to purchase homes that haven't been updated in years. The more dated the home, the more investors tend to net with appropriate updates—granite countertops, new appliances, floors, or whatever the home needs most.

Speculators and investors tend to make the most cosmetic changes to homes, and are known to tear out a kitchen and bath for replacement, too.

Long-term investors intend to buy and hold for rentals and tend to want to keep improvements at a minimum, so they will be much more interested in whether the home will cash flow as a rental property in its present condition or with minor cosmetic updates.

Retail or Wholesale. It's up to you and the way you present your home to the market. Investors tend to shy away from homes that have already been well-updated because the improvements have been priced into the market. A home in top condition will more likely attract a buyer who wants to live there than one who wants to flip the home.

Bargain Hunters. These are buyers who take advantage of softening prices and/or lots of inventory to make low-ball offers in the hope of getting a great deal on an older home. Sometimes bargain hunters are first-time home buyers who simply can't spend more for a home, and they are highly motivated to buy the most home they can possibly afford.

One way bargain hunters obtain property in neighborhoods they usually wouldn't be able to afford is to purchase a fixer-upper. They may be looking at their purchase as an investment, but unlike professional investors, they usually don't pay cash and don't have a crew on hand to do updates.

If your home hasn't been updated in years, the bargain hunter has to take into consideration the costs of paying someone else to remodel the home or doing the work themselves. Either scenario will take more off the price of your home than you may feel it deserves because the buyer may overestimate the costs of updates, or factor in a hassle line item for doing the work.

Homes that have been updated and well-maintained tend to sell for more and closer to listing price, most agents will tell you.

The Better-Deal Buyer.   These buyers may love your home but they're more concerned with beating you at some kind of game. It's like buying a home is a contest they want to win, and they win only if you (the seller) lose. You lose when you make too many concessions, don't get your price, or accept some questionable terms in order to sell your home.

The tip-off that you're working with a better-deal buyer is that they react unreasonably to the size, features, and price range a home like yours truly has. They see themselves as the only ones who are interested in your home, overplaying their position as buyers.

The Too-Good-to-Be-True Buyer.   This buyer seems to be the real thing, offers full or close to full price, with no strings attached. Only later, you find there's a problem: Their house is unsold, they're getting a divorce and no longer want the house, or they can't qualify for the loan.

Unfortunately for sellers, most state laws allow buyers out of contracts fairly easily. Working with your agent, you want to give buyers as little reason as possible to wiggle out of your deal by providing a beautiful home in great condition at a fair price.

The Motivated Buyer.   Motivated buyers are like treasures. This buyer is most likely to be represented by a real estate professional and is educated about the market. They will make reasonable offers and demands, and if they want you to make some kind of concession, there is usually a good reason why.

Keep in mind that even if an offer is lower than you were expecting, you can always counter. If you know your home is in tip-top condition, priced fairly, and should sell fairly quickly, there's no reason to allow yourself to be upset by buyers you know you will run across. You can't blame them for trying to get your home for less.

What's It Worth?

When considering your home's value in the marketplace, remember:

- *The value of your home relates to local sale prices.* The same home, located elsewhere, would likely have a different value.

- *Sale prices are a product of supply and demand.* If you live in a community with an expanding job base, a growing population, and a limited housing supply, it's likely that prices will rise. Alternatively, it's important to be realistic. If the local community is losing jobs and people are moving out, then you'll likely have a buyer's market.

- *Owner needs can impact sale values.* If owner Smith "must" sell quickly, he will have less leverage in the marketplace. Buyers may think that Smith is willing to trade a quick closing for a lower price and they may be right. If Smith has no incentive to sell quickly, he may have more marketplace strength.

- *Sale prices are not based on what owners "need."* When an owner says, "I must sell for $300,000 because I need $100,000 in cash to buy my next home," buyers will quickly ask if $300,000 is a reasonable price for the property. If similar homes in the same community are selling for $250,000, the seller will not be successful.

- *Sale prices are NOT the whole deal.* Which would you rather have: a sale price of $200,000 or a sale price of $205,000 but where you agree to make a "seller contribution" of $5,000 to offset the buyer's closing costs, pay a $2,000 allowance for roof repairs, fund two mortgage points, repaint the entire house, and leave the washer and dryer?

(Suggestions courtesy of REALTOR.com.)

Make It Easier on Agents and Yourself to Show Your Home

When you put your home on the market, you may feel you've invited the world to your doorstep. The phone starts ringing, and you may be asked by your agent to take the family and the dog for a drive while she shows your home.

Keeping the house show-ready can be a strain, but not if you follow the tips outlined in Chapters 3 and 4.

Don't Show Up for Showings

Among the reasons why you have an agent is to take your place for showings, but sometimes it just happens that you're home when another agent brings a prospective buyer.

Try to get out of the house, if possible, and take your pets and children with you, even if it's for a short drive to the ice cream shop.

First, do a five-minute pickup around the house. Assign each family member a room, hand them a basket that can be quickly shoved under a bed or put into a closet that can be used to gather up all stray clutter. When the showing is over, you can retrieve the baskets and put things in their proper place.

The main reason you want to be gone is that it allows the buyer the opportunity to imagine themselves as the new owners of your home. It also prevents you from inadvertently saying something that could improve the buyer's negotiating position.

Like preparing a witness for trial, your agent has probably coached you on what to talk about and what not to talk about when you come face-to-face with a buyer, but here are a few suggestions that may help:

- Stay off topics that could be sensitive such as churches, schools, or neighbors.

- Don't mention your pets, or your buyer's eyes might immediately start searching the floors for stains.

- Don't talk about what you've done to the home; that's a no-win game in which you either did too much and the buyer doesn't want to pay for it, or not enough and the buyer wants to discount your home.

- Don't mention warranties or guarantees. Some of these may be negotiation points you'll need later.

- Don't offer personal information about you, your situation, your job, or any family members.

- Don't mention other buyers or the number of showings you've had.

- Don't mention anything about the size of the house or its rooms. Again, it's a double-edged thing. "Cozy" rooms may appear small to some buyers, while some other buyers may be looking to downsize.

- It is your house, but the buyer may consider your presence an intrusion.

Should You Show Your Home During Holidays?

When you look at your November and December calendars, you may find the months already overloaded with seasonal obligations—shopping, entertaining, children's pageants, charity work, decorating the house, and so much more. If you are also trying to sell your home, you are under extra pressure to keep your home in showtime condition. And that could be the last thing you need before the holiday spirit is stretched too thinly.

It is understandable why you would be tempted to wait to market your home until after the holidays. You don't want to be faced with the possibility of packing and moving during the busiest time of the year. Besides, you can give your house a rest, and it will have better momentum after the holidays. Better to just pack it in and start fresh in January, right?

But wait! Jennie Ling, one of the top-producing real estate agents in Dallas, Texas, says taking your home off the market during the holiday season is a mistake. "The house sure isn't going to sell off the market!" Ling advises. "What is the advantage of that? So you're busy. Let your agent do the work. You can leave in the morning, go to work, go shopping, and let your agent take care of things."

Before you take your home off the market, consider the following points:

- Although buyer activity may appear to slow down, the buyers who are actively looking during the holidays are serious. The home market is no more affected than during other busy periods. If that were so, the market would shut down throughout the year as families concentrate on spring graduations, June weddings, summer vacations, and autumn back-to-school activities.

- Many buyers deliberately choose to shop for a home after the busy spring and summer rush. They know that it will be easier to look and that negotiations will be less stressful. This is particularly true of home buyers without children.

- Relocating families often don't have a choice in when they can leave for their new destination. Although 68 percent of transferring families have children, many families have to transfer during the middle of the school year. These families are that much more motivated to get their families settled in before the January semester begins or to arrange for the move during spring break in March. If you sign a contract by New Year's Eve, the timing couldn't be more perfect.

- At holiday time, our culture focuses on family and the home. Preparing for the indoor activities of winter is one of the most enjoyable periods of family life. Allowing buyers to view your home during this most hospitable of seasons lets them better picture their own family life in the attractive environment you have created.

- When is your home ever more beautiful and inviting? You have cleaned and decorated, and your home looks like a picture postcard. If the results are good enough for family and friends, they will surely be good enough to impress your buyers.

- With reduced inventories and motivated buyers, you will have all the members of the MLS on your team. You may find you have more showings than you would if you marketed your home during a busier time of the year.

- If you do get a contract, you can arrange the terms to suit your needs. If moving during the holidays isn't an option, you can put in the closing date of your choice.

Help! I'm Still Not Getting Offers!

Getting offers depends a lot on you and your motivation to sell. If you are being transferred, enlarging your family, or preparing to make an offer on another home, you are a motivated seller—ready to make the best deal to sell your home quickly.

Agents have a saying that when it comes to lack of offers the problem is always the same—price. But as you learned earlier, condition and location also impact buyers' considerations.

You and your real estate agent can take numerous and appropriate actions to help you meet your goals, including price adjustments and improvements that you've heard buyers would like to see in feedback. Once those are made, your agent will contact the buyers' agents to see if the buyers are still interested.

But many sellers aren't in a hurry to sell. They may want to test the market to see how high prices will go, and that gives the agent very little to work with.

The problem is that most buyers who are preapproved by a lender have a fairly narrow range to shop in. If you've overpriced your home, as you learned earlier, you have prevented the ones who are qualified to buy your home from ever seeing it, because they will have been taken to your competition instead, and may have already purchased a home.

Markets can change rapidly in many areas. When an agent gathers information for a seller, that data applies only to the current market. If the home has been on the market for a few weeks without an offer, a new group of competing homes could have joined the market that are more move-in ready or better priced than your home.

If your home isn't selling, it's time to review comparables again with your agent and consider lowering the price of your home or offering incentives to buyers if your state allows such transactions. Work with your agent to determine the next steps to take.

CHAPTER 8

Working the Buyer's Offer

The Purchase Offer

The sale agreement, or purchase offer, will be presented to your agent either by the buyer's agent or directly from the buyer if she is unrepresented.

The offer will include a price and the terms and conditions of the sale. Keep in mind that the offer is a firm contract when you agree to the price, terms, and conditions. If you don't agree and would like to negotiate, your agent will likely call the buyer's agent or buyer and let them know the sticking point. They may reach a verbal agreement over the phone or by fax, but it isn't a firm contract until all parties have signed and are in receipt of the signed copies. Keep the following in mind:

- Contracts routinely depend on the ability of a buyer to obtain financing, which is why most sellers prefer buyers with preapproval letters from lenders.

- A growing percentage of transactions involve a home inspection, or a physical review of the home, by a trained and independent observer.

- Lenders will establish numerous conditions before granting a loan. They will want a title exam, title insurance to protect against title errors, termite inspections, surveys, and an appraisal to assure that the home has sufficient value to secure the loan.

Real estate conveyances are state-regulated, with residential purchase agreements standardized by state or local real estate associations to comply with the provisions required by statutes.

The buyer's offer may include all or most of the following:

- Legal description (address) of the property.
- Sales price.
- Terms (cash, or subject to the buyer obtaining a mortgage).
- Contingencies—conditions in which the contract isn't binding if they aren't met, such as lender approval, major problem uncovered by inspection, and so on.

- Length of time of the contingency period (the time required to get lender approval, perform inspections, and for the seller to provide disclosures and perform repairs).

- Seller's promise to provide clear title (ownership).

- Seller's warranties and provision to keep property in good repair until buyer takes possession.

- Closing date.

- Amount of earnest money to accompany the offer (a deposit determined by the price of the home and local custom that is kept by the seller if the buyer defaults before closing).

- How the earnest money will be returned if the offer is not accepted or if some other contingency spoils the purchase, such as the home failing to pass inspection.

- Method by which real estate taxes, rent, and utilities, are to be prorated between buyer and seller.

- Type of deed.

- Provisions for who will pay for title insurance, survey, termite inspections, and so on (also determined by local custom and/or market conditions).

- Provisions for who will pay for repairs or retrofits.

- State required provisions such as contract subject to attorney review, disclosures.

- Provision for final walk-through inspection by buyer for closing.

- Offer expiration period.

■ Legal rights and attorney's fee provisions in the event of breach of contract.

The purchase offer will become a binding agreement if it is accepted as it is by the seller. If the seller wants to "work" the offer, by changing some terms such as the price or closing date, the contract is not binding unless the buyer accepts the new terms. If the seller crosses through the original offer and writes in the change with his initials, then he is providing a counteroffer. If the buyer agrees to the counteroffer and meets the terms by initialing the agreement, you have a binding contract that will move forward to the next step—meeting other conditions of the contract such as home inspection and the buyer's loan approval.

In some areas, offers and counteroffers are handled by attorneys, but in most states, your agent will help you facilitate the contract.

Is Your Buyer Qualified to Buy Your Home?

The first thing you want to determine when looking over an offer is its validity. Is this offer likely to close under these terms?

Unless the buyer who makes an offer on your home has the resources to qualify for a mortgage, you may not really have a valid contract, and the home won't sell. If possible, try to determine a buyer's financial status before signing a contract that takes your home off the market and out of consideration by other buyers. Use these five questions:

1. Has the buyer been preapproved for a mortgage? Such buyers will be in a much better position to obtain a mortgage promptly.

2. Does the buyer have enough money to make a down payment and cover closing costs? Ideally, a buyer should have 20 percent of the home's price as a down payment and between 2 percent and 7 percent of the price to cover closing costs.

3. Is the buyer's income sufficient to afford your home? Ideally, buyers should spend no more than 28 percent of total income to cover principal, interest, taxes, and insurance (PITI).

4. Does your buyer have good credit? Ask if he or she has reviewed and corrected a credit report.

5. Does the buyer have too much debt? If a buyer owes a great deal on car payments, credit cards, and so on, he or she may not qualify for a mortgage.

If you feel confident, move forward to consider the terms.

What's an Acceptable Offer?

According to REALTOR.com, the dream of every seller is to have a line of buyers outside the front door, each clutching higher and higher offers. And while this can happen, in most markets there is some balance between the number of buyers and sellers. A number of factors determine whether a buyer's offer is acceptable. They include:

1. Is the offer at or near the asking price? Is the offer above the asking price?

2. Has the buyer accepted the asking price or something close? Has the buyer then buried thousands of dollars in discounts and seller costs within tiny clauses and contract additions?

3. What is the alternative to the buyer's offer? If a home has not attracted an offer in months, then sellers need to determine if a better deal is possible—recognizing that each month costs are being incurred for mortgage payments, taxes, and insurance.

4. Does the owner have enough time to wait for other offers?

5. What if no other offers are received?

6. What if two offers are received? Do you choose the higher offer from the purchaser with questionable finances who may not be able to close, or a somewhat lesser offer from a buyer with preapproved financing?

In each case, owners—with assistance from their agents—will need to carefully review offers, consider marketplace options, and then determine whether an offer is acceptable.

Negotiating Techniques

Having the upper hand in negotiations depends on many variables including market conditions, how desirable your home is, and your flexibility or urgency.

As you learned earlier, buyers will tend to ask for more concessions in a buyer's market when there is lots of inventory to choose from and sellers are more conciliatory. In a seller's market, buyers are competing with other buyers and know they had better put their best offer on the table first. The thing to remember from your end is what you want to net versus the time, trouble, and expense of the items the buyer wants to negotiate.

That chandelier the buyer wants can be a bargaining chip, but not if the roof needs replacing. If the buyer wants you to replace a major item, you have to first think about whether the age of that item was factored into your price. Is what the buyer asks fair or is it too much? If you know your home is already priced under the market, throwing in a new roof is asking a lot. It could be that your buyer simply can't afford this home. If you want to stick with the buyer, there are other things you can do, such as offer seller financing. That way you, not the lender, collect the interest.

Seller Assist

Instead of giving the buyer a reduction in sales price, help them with closing costs. Savvy sellers will reserve their wiggle room for a true negotiation with a motivated buyer.

Seller subsidies, depending on the state where you live, can include decorating allowances, assistance with closing costs, and serving as the lender to the buyer.

"Even in the long haul, sometimes the $5,000 subsidy means more to the buyer than a $10,000 price reduction," advises M. Anthony Carr, *Realty Times* columnist.

Lenders limit seller subsidies because they would ideally like to see the buyer put more "money into the house," assuring they'll be less likely to default on a loan.

"Keep in mind how you word the cash that's being left at the table determines whether or not it is a seller subsidy," explains Carr. "If, for instance, after the home inspection it's determined the house needs a new roof and the seller agrees to fix it, this is generally not called a 'subsidy.' The seller is just agreeing to bring the house up to par. However, if the buyer requests $10,000 for a decorating allowance and then spends it on the roof, they have just negotiated a subsidy from the seller."

The wording and agreement in exchange of money is important in order to meet state laws governing the transfer of real estate, Carr cautions.

If the buyer seems to be demanding too much, or asking for repairs or replacements that you don't feel the price of your home justifies, you should think carefully about your need to sell to this buyer.

If you are moving into another home you've already purchased or you've been transferred, you might not be able to wait another month or two to complete a transaction with a different buyer. The opportunity cost might be more expensive than making the repair.

Some repairs, like replacing city-to-home gas lines, are extremely expensive and the home can't convey to a new owner unless you make the repair. Some lenders won't lend to a borrower if they are purchasing a home where the roof has been replaced by tacking a new roof over an older roof. So the nature of repairs also has to be considered. Is the repair, if it isn't completed, going to break the deal with this buyer and buyers to come?

Last, you must think about the long-term effects of negotiating over what could be a relatively small amount in hindsight.

"By the time the buyer and seller get to this point, my advice to both is to focus on the real goal," advises Carr. "Thus both buyers and sellers have to think about what will happen in the future if they don't go for the negotiation now. In a market moving up, the buyer should remember the next property is probably going to cost more than the one they are negotiating on right now. In a dropping market, the seller has to take into account the price drop and then the negotiations with the next buyer. A $1,000 negotiation may turn into $6,000 or more with a price drop and new negotiations in the future."

Is the First Offer the Best Offer?

The annals of real estate are well stocked with stories of sellers who refused to take a good, but not perfect, first offer, and who then waited a long, long time before finally accepting something else at a considerably lower price, says Bob Hunt, NAR Director for Orange County, California.

"A quick offer at near full price or full price doesn't mean your property was listed too low," says Hunt. "A low offer doesn't necessarily mean your home is overpriced."

In other words, don't second-guess yourself. Many buyers jump on new listings hoping that your urgency to sell will encourage you to accept the first offer that comes your way. They are working with agents or getting listing notifications from Internet sites, so don't be surprised at early bird offers. By the same token, you shouldn't expect offers to go up significantly with time.

"There often can be a transactional benefit to 'leaving something on the table,'" suggests Hunt. "A real estate transaction is a process. These days, with inspections and disclosures, there are almost always 'second negotiations' during the course of escrow."

Last, keep the feelings of all concerned in mind. "A buyer who feels ground down in the purchase negotiation may well be more difficult to deal with as other issues arise," cautions Hunt. You don't want to lose the sale over a skirmish.

Multiple Offers

It's a delightful position to be in—fielding multiple offers for your home. In California, for example, multiple offers are encouraged in some areas through the use of range pricing, where you set a minimum and maximum range you think your home is possibly worth. Since buyers don't know what other offers are being made, they might be inclined to put their best offers forward.

Different areas under different MLS rules have local customs for the handling of multiple offers. Your agent might announce a date for which offers will be read and one accepted. This puts bidders into a dueling match.

But sometimes a seller's market can backfire. If you price your home too high, you won't get as many offers. Also, consider down payment capability and motivation of the buyer, as well as appraisal and inspection contingencies (your home has to appraise at the bid-up price in order for the lender to lend money to the buyer).

Encourage the buyer to get an inspection report, for your own protection, even in a multiple offer situation.

CHAPTER 9

You've Got a Deal!
Preparing for Closing

The terms of your contract will outline which events will take place and when. While your buyer is working on finalizing financing, inspection, and closing issues, you are working on cleaning out the house, attending to any final requests by the buyer that you've agreed to, and making sure your title is in clear order by getting together your papers such as divorce documents, wills, or shared ownership titles.

You and your agent should make sure you have a few items nailed down that will make the transaction go more smoothly. In addition, your agent should give you some idea if you will have any costs at closing. While it's possible to close a transaction quickly, it's sensible to give both parties enough time to complete what they need to.

Select a Closing Date That Works for Everyone

Of particular interest to both of you is the closing date, because your schedules have to work out in four ways: You have to either be moved out or pay rent back to the buyer, and the buyer must move out of his or her home and into yours on the moving-in date that you can agree to. Closing dates are challenging to schedule because service providers must also be ready, although they may not personally attend, including your lender, the buyer's lender, real estate agents, transfer agents (in the event of a co-op purchase), managing agents (for condominium purchases), attorneys, and the title company representative.

Tip: Many closings don't take place on time. In order to save money, buyers prefer closings at the end of the month so that they don't have to pay for an extra month's rent, utilities, property taxes, association fees, and so on. However, the problem is that month-end closings strain the service providers, which could cause delays. It would be far less frenetic to schedule a closing in the middle of the month or at the first of the month.

Title, Closing, and Escrow Agents

Depending on local custom or agreement, a closing agent will be chosen by the buyer and his agent or the seller's to facilitate the closing. Also known as an escrow agent, the closing agent's job is to make sure that the contract stays on track—that needed documents arrive on time and directions are followed, including loan and appraisal documents, title company requirements including the survey, and the lender's and owner's title policies. Title companies or attorneys typically handle this part of the transaction.

Both you and the buyer want to be assured that every inch of the property you are conveying is yours to transfer ownership. That's why getting loan title insurance is important for the buyer's lender, and owner's title insurance is important for the homeowner. According to the American Land Title Association (ALTA), www.alta.org, as many as 25 percent of title searches find a title problem that is fixed before the insurance is issued. These problems typically include deeds, wills, and trusts that contain improper information; outstanding judgments or tax liens against the property; and easements.

In order to issue title insurance, the title company must search public land records for matters affecting that title, and many search the "chain" of title back 50 years, says ALTA. Title companies fix the problems and then issue the title insurance, but they may need proper documentation from you in order to clear title, such as release of liens, divorce decrees, wills, and other papers.

Because the seller is conveying the property, the seller typically pays for the title policy for the buyer.

Opening escrow with a title or escrow company means that the buyer has deposited funds with the title agent to move the deal forward, including "earnest money." The earnest money is given to the seller if the deal falls through for any reason not contingent in the contract. Its purpose is to pay the seller for lost marketing time.

"The title or escrow agent is supposed to be a neutral third party who handles the paperwork, money, transaction instructions, and other details of a home purchase or mortgage refinance," says Broderick Perkins, *Realty Times* columnist. "The companies hold onto and then exchange, disburse, and transfer deeds, other documents, and monies related to the transaction." This includes paying off existing loans against the property. The monies go through the escrow account, but the proceeds aren't disbursed until the escrow agent is satisfied that all is in order, including the buyer's deposit, title insurance, and search fees; lender's fees; agent's commissions; filing and transfer fees; notary, attorney, and courier fees; and much more.

These assorted costs are known as "settlement" costs, and they are duly recorded on the U.S. Department of Housing and Urban Development's HUD-1 Settlement Statement or a reasonable facsimile, which eventually discloses all of a housing transaction's costs for both the buyer and the seller, says Perkins. Both the buyer and seller should receive a copy of the settlement costs at least one day before closing.

Needless to say, a title or closing agent should be chosen carefully. Most real estate agents know which title agents are the most efficient and detail-oriented, but don't be afraid to ask for comparisons.

Title Insurance

Local custom and the type of seller determine whether the buyer or seller pays for title insurance. In most markets, because the seller is conveying title, it is customary for the seller (or seller's agent) to choose the title company.

A title policy is insurance you don't want to be without, but it can be costly—as much as 1 percent of the transaction, but what it ensures against is any cloud to a clear and free title that might occur because of incorrect information provided by the title company. The title company researches the chain of ownership to make certain that the seller has the right to sell and doesn't have someone else on the title of the home (such as a spouse) who isn't also on the sales contract.

Typically, the buyer will be responsible for obtaining the title policy for the lender, which the lender requires for protection of the mortgage. However, the seller will usually be required to purchase the owner's title policy, which is given to the buyer to ensure clear transfer of the title.

Five Things to Understand about Title Insurance

1. It protects the buyer's ownership right to your home both from fraudulent claims against your ownership and from mistakes made in earlier sales, such as a mistake in the spelling of a person's name or an inaccurate description of the property.

2. It's a one-time cost usually based on the price of the property.

3. It's usually paid for by the sellers.

4. There are both lender title policies, which protect the lender, and owner title policies, which protect you. The lender will probably require a lender policy (which the buyer pays for).

5. Discounts on premiums are sometimes available if the home has been bought within only a few years since not as much work is required to check the title. Ask the title company if this discount is available.

(Copyright 2006. Reprinted with permission from REALTOR® Magazine Online.)

Buyer Inspections

As mentioned in Chapter 7—On the Market—your buyer may want to have the house inspected by a professional home inspector. It's in your interest to have this done as quickly as possible, so you and your agent will negotiate when that will be done and how an inspection might impact the terms of the sale.

One way to prevent surprises is to have an inspection of your own before you put your home on the market, as discussed earlier in Chapter 7. If you do so, you should disclose to your buyer any findings and what was repaired, removed, or improved.

In some areas, buyer inspections are performed before the buyer makes an offer to the seller, so the seller already knows what to expect when receiving an offer. In other areas, however, the buyer doesn't have an inspection until after the offer contract is accepted by the seller.

What to Expect for the Buyer's Inspection

As you may recall from having your home inspected when you purchased it, the buyer has an option period after you sign the purchase contract to have your home inspected. The option period gives the buyer time to hire an inspector, have an inspection, and decide whether he or she wants to live with the findings, repair the noted items, or ask you to repair some items. No home is perfect, even newly constructed homes, and that's why buyers frequently condition their offers on the opportunity to examine what they're buying.

According to the American Society of Home Inspectors (ASHI), www.ashi.org, a home inspection is an "objective visual examination of the physical structure and systems of a home, from roof to foundation." Like a physical exam from a doctor, the home inspector examines what's visible, and if he finds anything worthy of discussion, he'll make an evaluation and recommend remedies.

The purpose of a home inspection is to give the buyer as much information about the condition of the property as possible. You can expect the home inspection to cover the structural elements of the home, including:

- Foundation.
- Roof.
- Brick, wood, metal siding, stucco, concrete form.
- Doors and windows.
- Electrical.
- Plumbing.
- Insulation.
- Appliances.
- Heat/air-conditioning.

Outdoor elements will also be inspected:

- Driveways, sidewalks.
- Other buildings to be conveyed with the property like garages.
- Porches, patios, balconies.
- Septic tanks.

Some inspections are more detailed than others, but not every defect will be visible to the home inspector, so he has to rely on experience to tell him if certain features of the home might cause the buyer problems. Certain appliances may appear in good working order but may also have a short life span. A roof may have a few good years left, but there's no way an inspector could know for certain how many.

Inspections are often used as negotiating tools, but that doesn't mean every item marked by the inspector has to be addressed by the seller. For example, you might have priced your home knowing that it "needed a little work," whereas you have no reason to discount or negotiate a home that is in top condition.

However, the outcome of a home inspection is as important to you as it is to the buyer, because it could cause your sale to go off track. You could also be in for big unexpected expenses, such as foundation work, replacing a major appliance, or plumbing.

If your buyer is going to ask you to repair any items, he or she should provide you with a copy of the inspection report. You can then discuss with your agent what should be done: Should you make the repair? Should you knock a little off the price of the home? Or should you ignore the request?

Just make certain that the report is from a legitimate home inspector with credentials such as membership in ASHI. Like NAR members, ASHI members adhere to higher educational and customer service standards that go beyond licensing requirements. (Not all states require licensure.)

Appraisals

Real estate values change constantly, necessitating the redetermination of current value whenever a property changes ownership or is refinanced. Lenders hire appraisers (even though the buyer pays for the appraisal) because they want to assess the risk of loaning money to buy a certain home.

The main consideration for the seller is that the home has to appraise at or above the purchase price in order for the lender to green-light the loan. To help the lender in her decision to lend the buyer money, the lender will dispatch an appraiser to your property. The appraiser's job is to render an "objective opinion of value" called a Uniform Residential Appraisal Report. Depending on his experience in the area, the appraiser will select comparable properties and look at the condition and features of your home. A lender's appraisal isn't used to determine market value; it is for the benefit of the lender to verify the property as security for the amount of the loan.

Lenders know that homes rise and fall in value, and because they can't see into the future any more than anyone else, they rely on current market value as the best criterion for determining risk.

Homeowner's Insurance

Lenders require buyers to have homeowner's insurance (often called hazard or fire insurance) on their new property, which takes effect immediately upon closing.

Due to the high number of claims over the past few years from mold to natural disasters like hurricanes, many insurers are limiting the number of new policies they write in a given area. In addition, the policies may be severely restricted, disallowing water damage claims that could lead to mold. In most locales, flood insurance is available only on a separate rider.

If you are selling a townhome, rowhome, or condominium, insurance is still required, but the kind of policy the buyer gets depends largely on the type of ownership they will have. In a cooperative type of home where the roof, amenities, and grounds are shared in common, the homeowner's association policy may cover exterior buildings and amenities, while the buyer may need only to purchase a policy to cover her possessions. The main point is that the buyer's agent, lender, and insurer are all in agreement about the type of home that is being conveyed.

The sooner buyers start shopping for homeowner's insurance the better, as most lenders will not fund loans without it, and many types of loans require homeowner's insurance to be escrowed, along with property taxes.

It's also important for you to call your homeowner's insurance company and let them know you are moving to a new home. If you already have your home picked out, they can arrange to transfer or alter the coverage very easily.

What Does Homeowner's Insurance Cover?

Homeowner's insurance covers what the policy says it covers, protecting the homeowner from financial losses due to storms, fire, theft, or other events. You must read the policy carefully, so there are no misunderstandings.

As many have found out, storm damage may not include flooding if the flood was found to come from another source. For example a hurricane may have blown the roof in, but flood waters may have ruined the first two floors of the dwelling. In that case, a homeowner's policy may not cover water damage, even though the events were related.

While you can purchase a policy that covers only the structure of your house and any outbuildings such as a detached garage or storage shed, you can also add other coverage:

- *Personal property.* This pays for household items such as furniture, jewelry, clothing, and appliances that could be damaged, stolen, or destroyed.
- *Liability.* This protects you against financial loss if you are found legally responsible for someone else's injury or property damage.

- *Medical payments.* This pays medical bills for anyone hurt while on your property.

- *Loss of use.* This pays living expenses if you have to move out of your home while it's being repaired.

- *Earthquake riders.* This pays for damages incurred from earthquakes.

- *Flood riders.* This pays for damages from floods.

Policies are approved by the state's Commissioner of Insurance. Some companies may sell more than one kind of policy. If you want more or less coverage, negotiate with your insurance company.

Why Does Homeowner's Insurance Cost More in Certain States?

Policy costs have a lot to do with the number and types of claims in certain states.

Insurers have access to a 10-year-old database called the Comprehensive Loss Underwriting Exchange Property Database (CLUE). This database tracks claims on properties and property owners. CLUE is a voluntary repository supplied by carriers of homeowner's insurance policies for the nation. It can tell an inquiring insurer the name and address of the policy holder, and whether there has been a claim for water, earthquake, tornado, fire, or other losses, and the damage claim amount paid. If the insurer thinks the house is a poor risk for another catastrophe, a homeowner's policy can be refused to the buyer, causing the buyer to look elsewhere for insurance.

Not only is the house subject to CLUE reports, but so is the policy holder. If you have had a number of claims, insurers might conclude that you are a poor risk, which will make it more difficult for you to get insurance on your next home.

The solution? Make claims to insurers wisely. Start shopping for insurance early for your next home. Notify your own lender as soon as possible who your insurance agency is and what kind of policy you purchased to make sure you have enough coverage to protect the lender so she will make the loan.

Richard Collier, vice president of marketing and sales for Choice-Point (www.choicepoint.net), and the developer of CLUE reports, says that they are an important tool for buyers and sellers, but cautions that they can't be used to check out properties. CLUE property reports can be obtained by the buyer concerning his own claims records, but the buyer cannot access the seller's report except through an insurance agency, which may say whether the home is insurable, or the seller.

CLUE property reports are accessible online at www.choice trust.com. Consumers can order one free CLUE report every 12 months.

Postcontract Pitfalls

Selling a home is like climbing Mount Everest: Getting a signed contract is a great accomplishment, but that's only half the journey. The typical home sale today involves more than 20 steps after the initial contract is accepted to complete the transaction.

Much of what needs to be done before the closing is the responsibility of appraisers, loan processors, attorneys, and inspectors. The agent's role is to coordinate those responsibilities, helping to ensure that others do their jobs promptly and correctly and that the closing isn't jeopardized.

Many steps between contract ratification and closing involve the cooperation of both buyer and seller, and attentive agents on both sides of the transaction will troubleshoot and keep everyone on track.

Home Selling from **A** *to* **C** *(Acceptance to Closing)*

Home Sellers

- *Select an escrow agent.*
  One of the parties selects an escrow agent. The escrow agent will collect the necessary documentation from each side and will conduct the closing.

- *Assemble condo or homeowners association (HOA) documents.*
  Sellers who live in condos or in a neighborhood subject to an HOA must provide financial statements and recent reports to the buyer for review.

Home Buyers

- *Deposit earnest money funds.*
  Earnest money funds are deposited according to instructions, which include who will hold the deposit, whether interest is to be accrued, and conditions of release. These funds are applied to the down payment at closing.

- *Finalize the loan application.*
  If interest rates are falling and more homeowners are refinancing, additional time may be needed to obtain a mortgage commitment. If the property is being financed with a VA, FHA, or other government-backed loan, it will be necessary to obtain copies of correctly filed building permits for all remodeling or additions done since the original construction. Decisions about locking in interest rates can be made at any time after a contract is ratified.

Home Selling from A *to* C *(Continued)*

Home Sellers

■ *Order a preliminary title report.*
A title search examines all public records to determine any defects in the chain of title; in other words, to confirm that the seller actually owns the property and has the right to transfer ownership.

■ *Request a satisfaction letter from present lender.*
Total amount due on any existing mortgages must be provided in advance of settlement.

■ *Coordinate home appraisal and inspections.*
Arrangements for access to the property must be made for the lender's appraisal and any inspections as specified in the contract.

■ *Arrange final utility readings and payments.*
When bills are prepaid, payments will be prorated at settlement between buyer and seller.

Home Buyers

■ *Order the home appraisal (this is usually handled by the lender).*
Lenders require an appraisal before committing to a loan. Appraisers compare the features and condition of a home to similar properties to arrive at a dollar figure for its value.

■ *Arrange the property survey.*
A survey determines the boundaries of the property, its location, and the size and shape of any buildings on the lot. The survey also identifies any existing easements or encroachments.

■ *Order inspections.*
Inspections may include those for home condition, radon, lead, earthquake, and termite infestations. Inspections should be ordered as soon as the contract is ratified so there is time to remedy any problems or renegotiate terms. Agents have established relationships with inspectors and contractors to help ensure that their transactions get priority in busy times.

■ *Verify employment and financial information.*
Lenders will require buyers to verify employment and financials before committing to the loan to ensure that there have not been significant changes since the process began.

(Continued)

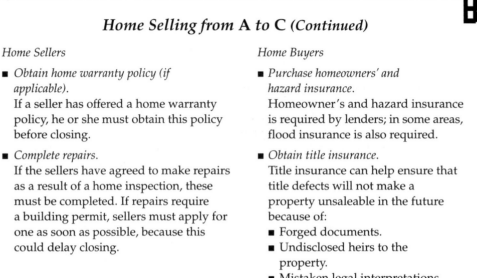

Home Selling from A to C *(Continued)*

Home Sellers

- *Obtain home warranty policy (if applicable).*
  If a seller has offered a home warranty policy, he or she must obtain this policy before closing.

- *Complete repairs.*
  If the sellers have agreed to make repairs as a result of a home inspection, these must be completed. If repairs require a building permit, sellers must apply for one as soon as possible, because this could delay closing.

- *Have an attorney prepare the deed.*
  The deed is the document by which the owner transfers title to the property.

- *Arrange for payment of transfer taxes.*
  Most states require a tax on transfer of property. This expense is most often the responsibility of the seller. Cities and local municipalities may also charge transfer taxes.

Home Buyers

- *Purchase homeowners' and hazard insurance.*
  Homeowner's and hazard insurance is required by lenders; in some areas, flood insurance is also required.

- *Obtain title insurance.*
  Title insurance can help ensure that title defects will not make a property unsaleable in the future because of:
  - Forged documents.
  - Undisclosed heirs to the property.
  - Mistaken legal interpretations of wills or trusts.
  - Misfiled documents—deeds, liens, mortgage satisfaction documents.
  - Confusion caused by similarities in names.
  - Incorrect marital status.
  - Mental incompetence.

- *Secure a loan commitment.*
  Lender notifies escrow agent of commitment and confirms settlement date.

- *Transfer utility accounts.*
  Utilities should be transferred into the buyers' names as of the date of settlement.

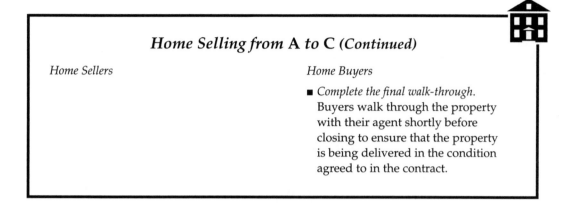

Home Selling from A to C (Continued)

Home Sellers

Home Buyers

- *Complete the final walk-through.* Buyers walk through the property with their agent shortly before closing to ensure that the property is being delivered in the condition agreed to in the contract.

CHAPTER 10

The Closing

The Contract Is in Force

After the option period is over, the contract is in force until closing, also known as "settlement."

The buyer has been busy getting the loan under way, their homeowner's insurance and their down payment together. Meanwhile, you're finished with repairs and any other final negotiations.

Depending on the custom in your market, you may allow the buyer one last opportunity to look at the home before closing, usually the morning of closing or the day before.

The Final Walk-Through

The final walk-through is where the buyer sees if the repairs and condition of the home meet expectations. For example, the utilities should be tested during the final walk-through, so be sure to leave the lights and gas on, and the plumbing turned on under your name until after closing.

To prepare for a final walk-through, make sure:

- Screens and storm windows are in place or stored.
- All appliances are operating.
- Intercom, doorbell, and alarm are operational.
- Hot water heater is working.
- Heating, ventilation, and air-conditioning (HVAC) are working.
- No plants or shrubs have been removed from the yard.
- Garage door opener and other remotes are available.
- Instruction books and warranties on appliances and fixtures are there.
- All personal items and all debris have been removed.
- All items that are included in the contract are present—draperies, lighting fixtures.

(Copyright 2006. Reprinted with permission from REALTOR® Magazine Online.)

Time Estimates for Delays

When things go wrong, closing can easily fall behind. Here's how much time to expect on particular delays:

One-Week Delays

- Buyer submits incorrect information to lender.
- Source of down payment changes.
- Escrow fails to notify parties about missing documents.
- Principals leave town without signing all necessary papers.
- Unknown defects are discovered in the property.
- Last-minute liens discovered.
- Cloud on title.
- Move-out date changes.

Two-Week Delays

- Lender decides at the last minute it doesn't approve of the borrower or the property.
- Lender raises interest rates.
- Lender requires last-minute reappraisal or repairs.
- Appraisal is too low.

Agents have extensive experience in handling problems that may arise during the time between contract and closing; they can anticipate difficulties and address them in time to ensure a smooth settlement for all involved.

What to Do If There's a Problem

If the buyer finds something wrong, that is not the time to delay the closing. Go ahead and attend, and make sure that you and the buyer's agents work out a way to address problems to everyone's satisfaction. A portion of the proceeds can be held in escrow until whatever dispute is solved.

What to Expect at Closing

You and your real estate agent will review that all the conditions of your purchase contract have been met, and that all directions to the closing agent have been given.

Depending on who's conducting the closing—in most cases, the title officer—you may be taken to a conference room. Sometimes the buyer's portion of the closing is scheduled separately.

Your portion of the closing costs will most likely be required to be in the form of a cashier's check. You'll be told how much you owe for:

- Sales commissions.
- Notary fees.
- Prorations of your share of costs for utilities, property taxes, and so on.

Prorations are costs paid on either a monthly, quarterly, or annual basis, such as homeowner's association fees or utilities, that you may have paid in advance or haven't paid yet. In some cases, you'll get money back for items you've paid in advance such as utilities or homeowner's association fees.

The buyer pays for his portion when he takes over ownership of the home for the remainder of the period. Assuming the buyer buys your home on the sixth of the month, he would owe the gas company for the remainder of the month, while you owe only for the first five days. The bill would be prorated for the number of days in the month and then each person would be responsible for the days of his or her ownership. (*REALTOR® Magazine*)

Closings that used to be quite simple are now complex thanks to a number of rules and regulations designed to protect consumers and other parties to the transaction. You may be surprised at the number of documents you have to sign, many of which are disclosures designed to protect all the participants at closing.

What to Keep after Your Closing

The Real Estate Settlement Procedures Act (RESPA) requires that you receive a statement, otherwise known as a HUD-1 statement, which itemizes all the costs associated with closing. You'll need this statement for income tax purposes and for any taxes owed when you sell your home.

The buyer will receive a deed that transfers ownership of the property from you to them, along with affidavits swearing to the various statements by either party. For example, you may sign an affidavit stating that you are the sole owner of the property and have not incurred any liens on the property.

Riders are amendments to the sales contract that affect the buyer's rights. If you've sold a condominium to a buyer, for example, you may have a rider outlining the condominium association's rules and restrictions to give to the buyer.

What Can Go Wrong

Most problems at closing can be prevented by good communication, particularly keeping the closing agent and seller informed of any changes that may impact the closing date.

According to a survey of 1,400 real estate agents in 2004 by Campbell Communications, about 12 percent of closings have to be rescheduled past the original closing date, and another 3 to 4 percent never make it to closing. The number one cause of the majority of these delays and lost deals, say about 73 percent of the agents surveyed, is due to "underwriting delays."

Other causes are also at fault for delaying closings, including "appraisal delays" (number two culprit) and "HUD-1s not available one day in advance of closing" (number four). The number three culprit is "Home buyer denied mortgage with initial lender." Thirty percent of agent respondents said, "Seller unwilling to extend closing for mortgage delays" and that is also a significant reason why home purchase transactions fail to close.

One side effect of not getting preapproved by a reputable lender is that if the buyer isn't able to qualify for the loan, the buyer may be denied, or put into a different loan product that carries higher closing costs. Many buyers are surprised to find themselves at the closing table with higher fees to pay.

Another problem is not knowing the requirements lenders have to close a loan. Certain lenders, particularly those working with Veterans Administration (VA) buyers and Federal Housing Administration (FHA) buyers, have stricter requirements for the working elements of the property like the air-conditioner and will use the inspection report and appraisal to issue a request to get a certain fixture or system repaired or replaced before the loan will fund. If the seller is unable to get the appropriate workpeople to complete the job, closing could be delayed. If this happens to you when you are selling your home, you must stay in close communication with your agent.

One of the most common problems is the lender finding a glitch on the buyer's credit report that must be addressed. For the buyer to arrange a payment or to find the appropriate paperwork and get it to the credit reporting agency in time is sometimes a challenge, particularly if the lender does a second credit check only a day or two before your closing date.

Buyers can also delay closing by trying to get a better mortgage interest rate just before closing, but lenders need time to process the loan, and they may be surprised to learn they pay more in fees or higher interest rates than if they'd stayed with the original loan.

Sometimes the closing agent will be forced to delay closing because many people want the same time period to close, usually the last couple of working days in the month. This is to avoid laying out more cash for prorations. Avoid closing agent schedule problems by scheduling the closing at the first or middle of the month.

The closing agent may have a role in controlling the closing day. Check with the escrow officer to get an idea of how long it will take to issue the title reports and how long it will take to prepare the closing documents.

Another way you can save time before your closing date is to ask for a brief appointment when you can review the closing documents in advance so that the closing agent can explain what each provision and commitment means and correct any mistakes.

As you learned earlier, many of these problems are preventable with good communication.

What Happens at Closing?

Closing—or "settlement" or "escrow" as it is known in some areas—is essentially a meeting where the closing agent (the party who conducts settlement) takes in money from the buyer, pays out money to the seller, and makes sure that the purchaser's title is properly recorded in local records along with any mortgage liens.

The closing agent reviews the sale agreement to determine what payments and credits the seller should receive and what amounts are due from the buyer. The closing agent also assures that certain transaction costs are paid (taxes and title searches).

What You'll Net at Closing

To find out how much money you'll net from your house, add up your closing costs and subtract them from the sale price of the house.

Closing Costs for Sellers	
Mortgage payoff and outstanding interest	
Prorations for real estate taxes	
Prorations for utility bills, condo dues, and other items paid in arrears	
Closing fees charged by closing specialist	
Title policy fees	
Home inspections	
Attorney's fees	
Survey charge	
Transfer tax or other government registration fees	
Brokerage commission	
Total	

(Copyright 2006. Reprinted with permission from REALTOR® Magazine Online.)

Closing is also the time when adjustments will be made. For instance, suppose you've prepaid taxes four months in advance. In this case, the closing agent will compensate you for the prepayment at closing by having the buyer pay you additional money.

This could also work in reverse. If you are behind on property taxes, the closing agent will reduce the money due to you at settlement by the amount of the unpaid taxes.

Understanding Capital Gains in Real Estate

When you sell a stock, you owe taxes on your gain—the difference between what you paid for the stock and what you sold it for. The same is true with selling a home (or a second home), but there are some special considerations and exemptions.

How to Calculate Gains

In real estate, capital gains are based not on what you paid for the home, but on its adjusted cost basis. To calculate this:

1. Take the purchase price of the home: This is the sale price, not the amount of money you actually contributed at closing.

2. Add adjustments:

   - Cost of the purchase—including transfer fees, attorney fees, inspections, but not points you paid on your mortgage.

- Cost of sale—including inspections, attorney's fee, real estate commission, and money you spent to fix up your home just prior to sale.

- Cost of improvements—including room additions, deck, and so on. Note here that improvements do not include repairing or replacing something already there, such as putting on a new roof or buying a new furnace.

3. The total of these is the adjusted cost basis of your home.

4. Subtract this adjusted cost basis from the amount you sell your home for. This is your capital gain.

Example of Calculating Gains

Let's say you've just sold your home, which includes a master bath upgrade, for $227,500. The following example, using the preceding guideline, shows you how much you would earn in capital gains:

Original purchase price	$130,000
Cost of purchase	$1,500
Cost of sale	$15,000
Cost of improvements	$20,000
Total (adjusted cost basis)	$166,500
Sale price	$227,500
Capital gain	$61,000

Please remember that this is an example only and should not be used as accurate data when you are calculating your adjusted cost basis.

Also, you should contact a tax professional to ensure that you are following the capital gains rules correctly. You can also visit the IRS web site at www.irs.gov for more information.

A Special Real Estate Exemption for Capital Gains

Since 1997, up to $250,000 in capital gains ($500,000 for a married couple) on the sale of a home is exempt from taxation if you meet the following criteria:

- You have lived in the home as your principal residence for two out of the past five years.
- You have not sold or exchanged another home during the two years preceding the sale.

Also note that as of 2003, you also may qualify for this exemption if you meet what the Internal Revenue Service (IRS) calls "unforeseen circumstances," such as job loss, divorce, or family medical emergency.

(Copyright 2006. Reprinted with permission from REALTOR® Magazine Online.)

Turning Over the Keys

Once both parties have closed, and the lender's money has funded the disbursements, the keys are turned over to the buyer, unless you and the buyer have made other arrangements.

You did it! Hopefully, with the suggestions in this book as well as from your agent, your transaction went smoothly. Now, it's time to celebrate, but there's more to do: Get ready to move to your next home.

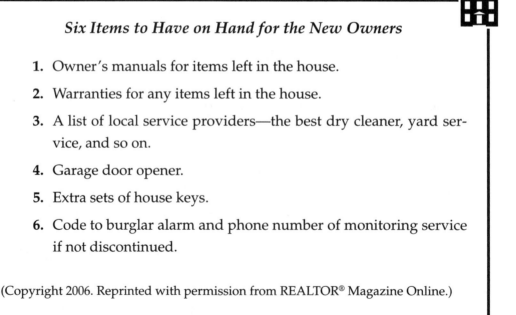

Six Items to Have on Hand for the New Owners

1. Owner's manuals for items left in the house.

2. Warranties for any items left in the house.

3. A list of local service providers—the best dry cleaner, yard service, and so on.

4. Garage door opener.

5. Extra sets of house keys.

6. Code to burglar alarm and phone number of monitoring service if not discontinued.

(Copyright 2006. Reprinted with permission from REALTOR® Magazine Online.)

CHAPTER 11

Planning a Stress-Free Move

Moving ranks as one of the most stressful events in anyone's life. Not only is the planning and preparation time-consuming and labor-intensive, but moving also takes an emotional toll on family members and even on pets.

According to a 2004 study released by Royal LePage Relocation Services (RLRS), a division of one of Canada's largest real estate companies, women experience more stress than men with nearly half saying they felt irritable, anxious, or had tension headaches and trouble sleeping. Only about one-third of men had similar complaints.

Children react emotionally, too, as they are facing leaving friends and family behind and wondering if they'll fit into their new school and activities. Pets can't talk, but they show their distress by hiding, chewing, neediness, accidents, or other out-of-the-ordinary behaviors.

There are many strategies you can follow to make moving as pleasant as possible for your family, the most important of which is to get started early, particularly if you are moving at a high-volume time like summer.

You can manage stress by doing the following as soon as you know for certain you will be moving:

- Take a complete inventory of everything you own, with photos. This will be helpful to insure your belongings for the correct amount both for the move and for your home-owner's insurance, and to help in case you need to make a claim.
- Get together all documentation of antiques, paintings, jewelry, and other valuables.
- Gather and file all warranties, instruction booklets, and receipts for appliances and electronics you'll be moving.

- Gather all sales materials, fliers, copies of contracts, credit reports, telephone numbers of workpeople, and everything associated with your move into one place so you can access it quickly and easily. You won't be needing most of these items right away, and they will be safely stored in a safety deposit box until you're ready to get them again.

- If you are moving into a gated community or a high-rise, find out what procedures you and your movers will need to follow, such as obtaining security clearances or using service elevators. Some movers charge extra for moves where there are stairs, split-level floor plans, or moves involving elevators.

- Most moves occur within 50 miles of the home buyer's previous home. Many items you will want to move yourself in your own vehicle, including your personal records, jewelry, or collectibles.

Moving Checklist

The following checklists will help you stay organized in the weeks leading up to your move.

Eight weeks before:

- Remove unnecessary items from your attic, basement, storage shed, and so on.

- Use things you can't move, such as frozen foods and cleaning supplies.

- Secure a floor plan of your new residence to help you decide what to keep.

- Start an inventory of your possessions. This is useful for insurance purposes as well as a review of what you have to move. Make sure to take pictures of things to document your ownership. If you have to file an insurance claim, these will be invaluable.

- Solicit estimates from at least three moving companies.

- Call your homeowner's insurance agent to find out to what degree your move is covered.

- Create a file for documenting all moving papers and receipts.

- Arrange to transfer your children's school records.

(Continued)

Moving Checklist (Continued)

Six weeks before:

- Contact your CPA for information about pertinent tax deductions.

- Evaluate your possessions inventory. Do you really need everything you have? Can you donate anything to charity?

- Notify your friends, relatives, professionals, creditors, subscriptions, and so on, about your move.

- Begin the off-site storage process, if applicable.

- Locate high-quality health care professionals and hospitals in your new location.

- Complete change of address via postal service cards or an online service for the following:

  - Banks.

  - Charge cards.

  - Religious organizations.

  - Doctors, dentist.

  - Relatives and friends.

  - Income tax bureau, Social Security Administration, union.

  - Insurance broker, lawyer, CPA, stockbroker.

  - Magazines (for assistance with this task, go to www.oneswitch.com).

  - Postal service.

  - Schools.

Moving Checklist (Continued)

- Clean your closets.

- Hold a moving/garage sale or donate items to charities.

- Choose a mover.

- Contact your mover to make arrangements and inquire about insurance coverage.

- If relocating due to a job, contact your employer to see what costs, if any, they will cover.

Four weeks before:

- Send furniture, drapes, and carpets for repair/cleaning as needed.

- Gather auto licensing and registration documents; medical, dental, and school records; birth certificates; wills; deeds; stock and other financial documentation.

- Contact gas, electric, oil, water suppliers; telephone, cable TV, or satellite TV; and trash collection companies for service disconnection/connection at your old and new addresses. Also ask for final readings.

- Request refunds on unused homeowner's insurance and prepaid cable service.

- Notify your gardener, snow removal service, and pool service, if applicable.

- Contact insurance companies (auto, homeowner's, medical, and life) to arrange for coverage in your new home.

(Continued)

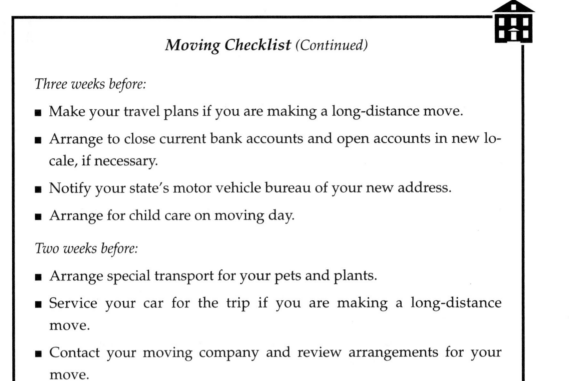

Moving Checklist *(Continued)*

Three weeks before:

■ Make your travel plans if you are making a long-distance move.

■ Arrange to close current bank accounts and open accounts in new locale, if necessary.

■ Notify your state's motor vehicle bureau of your new address.

■ Arrange for child care on moving day.

Two weeks before:

■ Arrange special transport for your pets and plants.

■ Service your car for the trip if you are making a long-distance move.

■ Contact your moving company and review arrangements for your move.

Moving with Children

Only you know if certain family members are going to take a move well or not, and you can tailor your approach accordingly, but in most cases, the sooner you tell everyone the better.

Children need time to process big changes, not the least of which is the feeling of the loss of control over their lives. There are many ways you can help.

- Attitude is infectious: If you're happy about the move, your child will have a difficult time being unhappy for long.

- Use the Internet, books, and other media to educate your child about where you're going.

- A move is the same to a child whether it's one mile or one thousand miles away. Be sensitive to your child's sense of helplessness that he won't be able to walk next door to his best friend's house anymore.

- Focus on activities your child will want to continue or try, but don't expect enthusiasm quite yet. Perhaps your daughter is on a soccer team; show her that you are researching soccer options at your next home. Contact the schools and recreational parks in your new area to set up an appointment where your child can meet her new coach and teammates before the move.

- Emphasize how and when you'll stay in touch with old friends. Whether it's through e-mail, a cell phone free long-distance plan, or personal visits, let your child know you are thinking of these things for him.

- Let your child have some control over her new environment. If she wants to paint her room purple and that's helping her look forward to the move, well . . . it's just paint, isn't it? You can live with it.

- Contact your child's new school and find out if there is a teacher's blog or chat room that the kids use, where your child can get acquainted online with her new teachers and classmates.

- Remember that change is harder for some children than for others. Be sensitive to mood swings. They are a normal expression of fear, frustration, and even anger.

- Help your child pack his belongings, starting with items he won't need at first, such as winter clothes. As he gets used to making decisions about what to keep and what to donate or throw away, he'll adjust to the idea of moving, and may begin to look forward to it. Needless to say, favorite items such as books or toys should stay with the child.

- Bank on things you'll do when you get to your new home. If having a home of your own means you'll have a dog for the first time, let your child search the Internet or books for information about breeds of dogs or training materials.

- It can take up to about 16 months for adults and children to adjust to a move. Don't expect them to be acclimated before you are!

Something fun you can do with your whole family is to make large, easy-to-read copies of your new floor plan (if you don't have one, you can draw one from memory to scale) and give each family member a copy so they can plan their furnishings for their new rooms.

Take measurements of your furnishings so you'll know in advance if that table fits where you plan it to go. As you decide what goes where, make notes on your master floor plan so you'll remember where things go on moving day.

You can also use the floor plans to discuss with your family what to keep and what to move. This will save you time later as you try to edit your belongings to your new home. In many cases you'll have more room, but if you are scaling down some tough decisions have to be made.

The sooner you start donating or throwing unwanted items away, the less you will have to do as moving day approaches. Do a little each day, even if it's only to pack and mark one box and throw out one garbage bag of junk. You'll be surprised how quickly your efforts will add up.

To Have a Yard Sale or Not to Have a Yard Sale

As we discussed in Chapter 3, yard sales are a good way to remove the clutter in your home. They are also a good way to get rid of items that you really don't want to move. So you may want to consider having a yard sale right before you move to your new home.

While yard sales are not the most entertaining way to spend a weekend for some people, for other people yard sales are fun.

Here are some suggestions on how to make a yard sale work for you.

- Ask neighbors to join in. They can help man the event, as well as pay for advertising.

- More stuff means more customers. Even with the competition from your neighbors' stuff, you'll have plenty of business.

- This is a great way to get rid of stuff you don't value anymore, or stuff that's hard to get rid of—like old computer monitors.

- Make sure you have a permit, if you need one, or all your profits may go to paying fines.

A better alternative for most people is to donate their unwanted goods. The advantage to this is that you'll be able to deduct the full value of the item, according to tax laws, as opposed to taking pennies on the dollar. Plus, things you are ready to discard are greatly appreciated by others.

Charitable organizations often have moving trucks that can pick up large items. However, you should check with the organization you want to donate to and make sure it can pick up your items. You may have to schedule this two to three months in advance to ensure pickup before you move.

A third option is to sell the items on eBay or similar web sites, but that could cause you to have to stop other activities in order to ship items to buyers. Another alternative is to deliver the unwanted items to a local eBay store or consignment store to sell for you. That way you're thinking about them, handling them, and moving them only one time.

Remember, anything you don't give away, throw away, or donate, you're going to have to move. Moving companies estimate moves by the room and by the pound, so ask yourself frequently, is that item worth paying to move?

If you need window coverings for your new home, they may take weeks to order, so be sure to plan ahead and have them ordered and installed between closing and your moving date if at all possible.

You'll also want your utility hookups to take effect after closing so that workpeople will be able to use the electricity and water. Also, arrange for the type of Internet connection you want, as well as cable or satellite TV. You may find that your cable service doesn't extend to your new home, and you may have to make other arrangements to get TV service.

You should fill out a change of address form with the postal service. Also, inform your bank and creditors so that you aren't penalized if a bill fails to show up in time for you to pay.

Save a master floor plan for the movers so they will know exactly where to move your things. Movers don't have time to memorize complicated color codes, so it's easier to simply mark boxes clearly with the room and level where you want them to go. This helps them load their trucks more efficiently for multiple-storied homes. Furniture pieces can be tagged with directions so they will know at which wall to place the beds, the couch, and the breakfront.

Choosing a Moving Company

Referrals are a great way to find movers. If you know people who have moved recently, ask them if they were pleased with their mover. Your real estate agent deals with people moving all the time—she'll know who's good, too. But be open to getting referrals in other places. Storage facilities are a great place to get referrals because people use movers to move their things to storage. They know who does a good job.

Most major moving companies, even if they are local, have web sites where you can visit and compare information, so do your research. There are also a number of online sites that provide company information and online quotes, such as REALTOR.com and www.moving.com. You can also check the American Moving and Storage Association at www.moving.org for a variety of moving resources. As mentioned earlier, it is wise to get at least three quotes from movers. All of this collective information will help you choose the moving company that best suits your needs and budget.

Moving dates and closing dates don't have to be on the same day. It may serve you better to close earlier than you plan to move so that you'll have time to paint, install new carpet, or make other updates before you move to your new home.

During peak periods especially, such as summers and weekends, movers need plenty of notice, so start looking for a mover as soon as you know for certain you are ready to move. They may also cost more during peak periods or charge a higher hourly rate on weekends or holidays.

According to REBAC, NAR's buyer's agent affiliate, peak periods include:

- The beginning and the end of each month, since this is when most closings take place.
- All holidays, but especially those where school vacations coincide.
- Summer months, since the majority of families will try to orchestrate a move between the end of one school year and the beginning of the next.

Moving companies will give you an estimate either over the phone or in person, according to the number of rooms of furniture you have and the number of floors you are moving out of or into. Ask for a written estimate and whether the estimate is binding, which means it's good for your moving date. You should also know how many movers you are being charged for. Make sure the mover is bonded and insured; a worker could get hurt while loading boxes, or one of your items may get damaged.

If your move is out of the area, your estimate will be based on the distance of your move and the projected weight of your shipment, rather than an hourly rate. In that case, you need to be even more careful about the amount of items you want moved.

Make sure the mover inspects each room for furniture and loose objects that will be transported, as well as storage areas at the house such as the attic, garage, basement, and outbuildings. The mover will need to view everything that will be going to the new location in order to provide you with an accurate estimate.

Moving is labor-oriented, so there is a wide range of services that you can take advantage of, including:

- *Packing and unpacking.* Are you willing to do this yourself, or would you prefer to pay professionals to pack some or all of your loose materials?

- *Boxes.* Most movers will sell you new boxes, and the prices will vary per company. Ask about used boxes, since some movers will allow you to drive to their site and select previously used boxes that remain with the company after moves are completed. If you will need a lot of boxes, gathering used ones will represent significant cost savings.

- *Special handling.* If you have unique pieces (like a piano), heavy pieces (e.g., woodworking machinery), or very delicate pieces (e.g., antiques), you might need a special quote that identifies special handling of the object.

- *Special packaging.* The movers may recommend that certain pieces be packed in wooden crates. Check the cost versus the advantages of this decision.

- *Insurance.* Most movers have some level of liability insurance that covers their moves. However, it is worth investigating additional insurance since it is not uncommon for objects to be damaged during the move.

(Source: REBAC Homebuyer's Toolkit. Copyright 2006.)

While price might be your major issue, you may also have to consider whether your move can fit into the mover's schedule. Your mover of choice may not be available when you want, or your items may need to be left in storage until the mover can deliver them. You also have to consider whether you are comfortable hiring a particular company. This is where talking to past customers will help. Contact the Better Business Bureau or the state attorney general to see if there have been any complaints against the company.

The person who is providing the estimate will usually be your contact at the moving company and during the move. Is she experienced, confident, a good communicator, and seemingly interested in satisfying your needs? In short, is she someone that you feel you can work well with during a stressful time?

If so, you've found the right company.

Easy Packing Tips

Buy lots of commercial grade tape, black markers and/or large labels, and plastic bags for liquid items such as detergents and shampoos. You can buy professional grade boxes, or pick up strong boxes at your local grocery, liquor, or electronics store. Ask other people you know who have just moved. See if you can take empty boxes from your workplace to use for packing.

The smaller the box, the heavier the items should be. The bigger the box, the lighter the contents should be. If possible, mark "heavy," "breakable," or other clues on the box, so they won't be improperly stored. Packed items should not exceed about 30 pounds. Be sure to cushion the bottoms and sides of the boxes with packing materials before putting breakables inside.

More tips:

- Thoroughly wrap all sides of breakables, with extra padding for spouts, lids, arms, and stands.

- Tape electrical cords to the underside of electronics. Do not tape furniture drawers closed, as tape can leave residue that causes damage.

- Do not pack combustibles, flammables, corrosive liquids including household cleaners, jewelry, and important papers or medicines.

- Do fill a box on moving day with essentials like toilet paper, paper plates, coffee maker and supplies, hand tools and extension cords, and cleaning supplies.

Tax Tips for Sellers as Next-Home Buyers

In Chapter 10, we covered some of the tax advantages for sellers. But as a next-home buyer, you may find that there are some deductions you can take on this year's income tax return. They include any prepaid mortgage interest and property taxes (consult your closing statement).

Points paid at the time of closing represent additional mortgage interest and may be taken as a deduction.

Many of your other closing costs are simply added to your cost basis for the property, so that when you sell, they will reduce the amount of capital gain you may have. Under current law, you do not owe tax on capital gain up to $250,000 ($500,000 for a married couple both of whom satisfy the residency test) that is received as a result of the sale of a home in which you have resided for two of the previous five years. Make sure to keep all of your records, however, including those for permanent improvements, which will also be added to your cost basis. You never know when Congress will change the law in the future, and these records may save you considerable money in tax owed.

On each year's income tax, you may deduct all property taxes paid on any real estate you own. You are also entitled to claim as deductions all mortgage interest paid on a first and second home. Your deduction is limited to interest on any amount up to $1 million borrowed to buy or improve your property, and interest on an additional $100,000 in equity loans or second mortgages. If your borrowing exceeds that amount, consult an accountant and an estate planner.

Moving Expenses

Many of your moving expenses can be deducted from your income taxes if your move is related to a job transfer or new job at least 50 miles farther from your old home than the old job was. Members of the armed forces also qualify for deductions when they are transferred to new stations.

Deductions are for one-way trips, and include:

- Packing, crating, and transporting household goods and personal effects for your entire household.

- Mileage for use of your own car in moving goods, yourself, or members of your household (or alternatively, actual gas and oil expenses).

- Tolls and parking fees paid during the trip.

- Storing and insuring household goods and personal effects for up to 30 days.

- Disconnecting and connecting utilities.

- Shipping of cars and pets.

- Transportation and lodging (but not meals) for yourself and members of your household while traveling to the new home.

Settling In

While it's tempting to get everything squared away quickly, there's more to your new home than putting your belongings neatly in place. You want to feel at home as soon as possible, and that includes becoming part of your community.

Save some of the unpacking for a rainy day, and get outdoors for some fun and exploration. Make a game of it with your family. Let everyone go to the Internet, find your new city or town, and pick out something fun to see or do that the entire family can enjoy. Buy tickets to a sporting event. Visit the zoo. Tour galleries and furniture stores to pick out one great new piece for your new home. Find the nearest coffee shop or watering hole. Get on your bikes and ride around your new neighborhood. Find out where the local dog park is and let your dog make some new friends (and you, too). Sign up for an exercise class, dance lessons, or a golf clinic. Try something new that your new community is known for. If you've moved to a college town, sign up for a lecture series. If you've moved to the country, try horseback riding. Get a season subscription to the community theater.

Don't wait for your formal rooms to be perfect before you invite your new neighbors over. If you're in a high-rise or community with a club room, meet new people by taking your favorite card or board games to the common area. Take your dog for a walk around the neighborhood—dogs know how to make friends!

Join the school PTA. Offer to assist on the next school fund-raiser and to help the coaches of your child's teams with drinks, snacks, paperwork, stats, or whatever the team needs.

Moving can indeed be stressful, but it can also be a wonderful opportunity for learning, growth, and doing what you love. Happy moving day!

Conclusion

Selling your home does not need to be an intimidating experience, especially if you understand the home selling process. Whether you are upgrading or downsizing your living arrangements, getting the best deal for your home should be your primary goal. The NATIONAL ASSOCIATION OF REALTORS® encourages you to work with a real estate professional to ensure a smooth transaction when selling your home.

Home Seller's Glossary

ABR® Accredited Buyer's Representative. A designation held solely by REALTORS® who have met the educational and practical requirements demonstrating skills and knowledge to represent home buyers. Awarded by the Real Estate Buyer's Agent Council (REBAC).

adjustable-rate mortgage (ARM) A mortgage with an interest rate that changes, based on a specific index, after a predetermined number of years.

agency Any relationship in which one party (agent) acts for or represents another under the authority of the latter.

From REBAC's 2006 Homebuyer's Toolkit. Copyright 2006.

amortization schedule   A timetable showing the amount of each mortgage payment applied to interest and principal and the remaining balance after payment is made.

annual percentage rate (APR)   The cost of a mortgage stated as a yearly rate; includes such items as interest, mortgage, and loan origination fee (points).

appraisal   A qualified appraiser's written analysis of the estimated value of a property.

biweekly payment mortgage   A mortgage requiring payments every two weeks rather than the standard monthly payment. The benefit for the borrower is a substantial savings in interest over the life of the loan.

broker   A person who, for a commission or a fee, brings parties together and assists in negotiating contracts between them.

capital gains   The profit obtained from the sale of an asset, such as real estate.

certificate of title   A statement provided by a title company or attorney stating that the title to real estate is legally held by the current owner.

closing   A meeting at which a sale of a property is finalized.

closing costs   Expenses incidental to a sale of real estate, such as loan fees, title fees, appraisal fees, and so on.

collateral   An asset (such as a car or a home) that guarantees the repayment of a loan.

commission The fee charged by a broker for providing services related to a real estate transaction, such as marketing the property (for the seller), finding a property (for the buyer), and negotiating a purchase contract.

cost basis The original price paid for an asset such as real estate, including any commissions or fees, used to determine capital gains or losses at the time of sale.

deed The legal document conveying title to a property.

earnest money A deposit made by potential buyers to demonstrate their good faith interest in purchasing a property.

equity The difference between the current market value of a property and the amount owed on the mortgage(s).

escrow A deposit of value, money, or documents with a third party to be delivered upon the fulfillment of a condition. For example, the earnest money deposit is put into escrow, held by the broker, bank, or other party, until delivered to the seller when the transaction is closed.

Fair Credit Reporting Act A consumer protection law that regulates the disclosure of consumer reports by consumer/credit reporting agencies and establishes procedures for correcting mistakes on one's credit record.

good faith estimate An estimate of closing costs associated with the purchase of a home.

home inspection A thorough examination that evaluates the structural and mechanical condition of a property.

home warranty   A guarantee for mechanical systems and appliances, but not the structure, against repairs not covered by homeowner's insurance; coverage is for a specific period of time.

lien   A legal claim against a property that must be paid before the property can be sold.

loan-to-value (LTV)   The ratio of the amount of a mortgage loan to the appraised value or sales price of the property mortgaged, whichever is lower.

lock-in   A lender's written guarantee of a specified interest rate if a mortgage is closed within a set period of time.

mortgage   A loan secured by real estate. A mortgage is used by a borrower to pledge real property to the lender as security for a loan.

mortgage insurance   A contract that insures the lender against loss caused by a borrower's default on a mortgage.

net worth   The combined value of all of a person's assets, including cash, minus all debts and liabilities.

PITI   Principal, interest, taxes, and insurance: four components of a monthly payment on mortgage loans.

PMI   Private mortgage insurance: coverage provided by a private mortgage insurance company to protect lenders against loss if a borrower defaults. Coverage is usually required for a loan with a loan-to-value (LTV) percentage in excess of 80 percent.

point One percent of the amount of the mortgage. Lenders charge borrowers a percentage of the loan amount equal to the number of points to cover the lender's costs. Sometimes borrowers pay higher points in exchange for a lower interest rate.

prime rate The interest rate that banks charge to their preferred customers.

principal The amount borrowed or remaining unpaid on a mortgage loan.

real estate agent A person licensed to negotiate and transact the sale or purchase of real estate on behalf of a property owner or buyer.

REALTOR® The registered collective membership mark that identifies real estate professionals who are members of the NATIONAL ASSOCIATION OF REALTORS® and subscribe to its strict Code of Ethics.

REBAC The Real Estate Buyer's Agent Council, a wholly-owned subsidiary of the NATIONAL ASSOCIATION OF REALTORS® whose purpose is to educate and support real estate professionals and to promote superior buyer representation.

sales contract Also known as a purchase agreement, the legal document that details the price and terms of a property sale between a seller and a buyer.

settlement statement A document prepared by a broker, escrow company, or lender, detailing the complete breakdown of the costs and disbursements in a real estate transaction.

survey   A drawing or map showing the precise legal boundaries of a property and the precise location of improvements, easements, rights of way, encroachments, and other physical features.

title search   A check of public records to ensure that the seller is the legal owner of the property being sold and that there are no liens or other claims against the property.

Truth in Lending   A federal law that requires lenders to fully disclose, in writing, the terms and conditions of a mortgage, including the annual percentage rate and other charges the borrower will incur.

underwriting   The lender's process of evaluating a loan application to determine the risk of providing the applicant the requested funds.

walk-through   A final inspection of a home before closing to verify that the condition of the property and contents is as contracted.

Index